The
Lay
of the Land

A View from the Prairie

Brent Olson

J&LLeeCo.
Lincoln, Nebraska

Copyright © 1998 Brent Olson
Photos by Brent Olson
Back cover photo by Robin Olson

5432
Printed in the United States of America

ISBN 0-934904-36-7

J & L Lee Co.
P.O. Box 5575
Lincoln, NE 68505

www.binary.net/leebooks/

e-mail: leebooks@binary.net
1-888-655-0999

To my wife and children.
They not only give me something to write about,
but a reason to live.

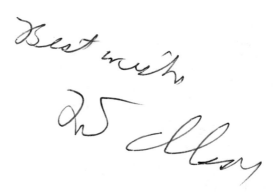

Contents

In Praise of Small Pleasures

The horses got out this morning at about 5:00 AM. Someone who shall remain nameless had forgotten to turn on the electric fence. We struggled out of bed when we heard the hoofbeats outside our window. My wife's ankle injury limited her to standing on the sidewalk making encouraging noises while I rounded them up.

Rounding up our horses in the night is not as hard as it might sound. They galumph around, taking divots out of the lawn and proclaiming to the night that they are sporty, wild, and free, that their daylight domesticity is just a sham. After they tire of this, they allow themselves to be caught and led back into the corral for a snack and a drink of water. So much for freedom.

We went back into the house. The night was unseasonably cold and my wife's grandmother's quilt was just right on the bed. I tried to sleep for another hour then got up.

I drove for two hours into a sunrise that in a reasonable world would have an admission charge attached, just for the privilege of watching it. The landscape was a sea of muted browns, blues and greens, with an occasional splash of the pure white of a pelican or heron searching the shallow sloughs for something to eat. A slight mist rose off the warming land.

As I drove I mused on the pleasure of sleeping with someone. I'm not talking sex here. I'm way too much a Minnesotan to feel comfortable talking about sex. I mean the pleasure of sharing body heat on a cool night with someone whose body heat you've been sharing for a quarter of a century.

I was on my way to pick up my number two daughter at camp. I arrived early, in hope that we could leave early so I could get back for my wheat harvest. On the way home she chattered about the camp, the horse she had ridden, and a stable boy. She sang the camp songs and she read to me from a book of poetry. Of our three children she is definitely her mother's daughter, and while their close relationship is warming to watch, I am sometimes a bit envious of it. I reveled in this time together.

All the way home I saw farmers out checking their fields, trying to decide if the wheat was ready. We have had rain for two weeks, stopping harvest, and everyone was getting a bit testy. There is a very narrow moisture range where wheat is harvestable and stable enough so it won't rot in storage. If you wait too long for it to dry, it may rain again and ruin the crop completely. It is not unheard of for an entire year's crop to be lost to indecision or bad luck.

When I arrived home I checked my wheat, biting into a few kernels and staring pensively at the horizon. It may sound unscientific, but I have a neighbor who didn't need to buy a moisture tester until he got dentures. I decided to go.

There is nothing on a farm more satisfying than combining. I can harvest about 400 bushels of wheat an hour. That's about enough wheat for 24,000 loaves of bread, every hour. You can't beat that for job satisfaction.

Early in the evening the combine began to malfunction. The header, that part of the combine that cuts the wheat off and directs it into the bowels of the machinery for processing, began to bob up and down uncontrollably. There was nothing to do but drag out the owner's manual.

The owner's manual is actually four loose-leaf books, totaling about 700 pages. Imagine one of Stephen King's long novels, only with diagrams, then try and find one certain paragraph in one chapter. It's not impossible, but it isn't quick.

I have a confession to make. I love troubleshooting charts. Do you know what I'm talking about? Most complicated machinery has them. You know, language like, "If the blendic is nurbling, check and see if the nurbling is farsst. If not, look for bllinggers. If bllinggers are not visible, the problem is probably in the ferndoggle."

You look through the charts until you find the specific problem you have, and are led to answer various questions until the solution to the problem becomes obvious. I love them because they are an effort to impose clarity and order in a very murky world.

Like I said, I love them, but do you know what I like better? When they are wrong.

More accurately, when they are wrong and I discover the mistake and fix it myself.

That happened tonight. If you are interested, the automatic header control module, which controls the electro-hydraulic height adjustment began to malfunction. I wasn't using that feature, that's only for soybeans, but the manual didn't mention that even turned off, it was still in the circuit. I figured that out for myself, sneered "HAH" at the world of engineers who can't even write a decent troubleshooting chart, cut that module out of the circuit and got back to work.

I arrived home very late. We have a grape arbor, built for us by a Russian physicist who was sorry he wrecked our car (long story). I've been tending the grapes for years with very little success, western Minnesota not being prime grape growing country. I think every one else had given up on them but this year for the first time we had a bumper crop of grapes, and when I got home from combining I had a sandwich made from grape jam made by my wife and daughter, from our very own grapes. It was delicious.

The unseasonable chill in the air was long gone and the house was warm as I walked upstairs, headed for a hot shower and cool sheets.

It was a good day.

Maybe better than good.

Love Songs from a Peasant

My father has a cousin who is big into genealogy. He went back to Norway and traced our ancestry back over 400 years. You know what he found? Four hundred years of peasants. No kings, noblemen, or even any prosperous merchants. Just a bunch of guys wearing comfortable shoes grubbing a living out of the dirt. The first tuxedo in the entire male lineage was worn by my son this year when he went to the prom.

The first year we farmed was 1976. It was the worst drought in thirty years. We started the year with nothing and ended it with less. My wife went to work as a secretary. We worked harder. In 1977 our first child was born. We are still here.

I like to think that this history gives me some credibility when I talk about farming. This does not mean I speak for farmers. In my experience, no one has the right to speak for farmers. We are all so different. Some of us farm because there is nothing else we can do. Some of us farm because we never knew anything else. Some of us farm because we are planning on making big money at it and some of us don't care about the money as long as our kids have kittens and sheep to play with and don't have to worry about gang fights.

I could say that we are all tied together with a love of the land and a response to a higher calling, namely feeding hungry people. I could say that, but it would be a lie. I know a lot of guys that don't love the land all that much. They'd let the whole state of Minnesota wash down to New Orleans, killing every fish and clam on the way if it would brighten up their bottom line. We are not all simple sons of the soil. Quite a few of us would think highly of conspicuous spending, not to mention oppressing some workers if we had any. I've got a neighbor who speaks longingly of getting a family of illegal immigrants for slaves.

No, I can only speak for myself. I live in the house my great-grandparents built. They built it ten years after they built the barn (priorities).

I am a third-generation democrat, with a small d. I think any unit of government above the level of a township board is basically a joke. I distrust big corporations, big unions, big government, and any farm organization that sends its leadership on expenses paid "fact finding trips" to interesting parts of the world. I belong to a lot of organizations, and serve on quite a few boards, but only ones that impinge on my life or affect my family.

I lose sleep over soybean prices, starving babies in Haiti, and whether or not my daughter will get the part she wants in the school play. The first breath of air I take when I step out of the house in the morning is as sweet as perfume, as long as the breeze is blowing towards the hog houses. I think that as a breed we farmers spend way too much time complaining and asking for help. I am going bald, have ulcers, and a line of credit that is seriously stretched. My town is shrinking, my friends are going broke, and our church needs a new parking lot and a lot more members.

I wouldn't trade places with anyone in the world.

Springtime

I think it is spring. Different people define spring differently. I once had a neighbor who decided when to plant corn based upon whether or not he could drop his coveralls and sit down in his field comfortably with his bare derriere on the plowed ground. I don't know how scientific this was, but I do know the neighbors tried to avoid the road past his place the first two weeks in May.

A lot of people get fired up by the first robin they see. I don't buy that. I've seen too many robins up to their little giblets in April snow to have much faith in their weather forecasting ability. Birds have brains about the size of a wad of chewing gum. I would sooner believe a government economist.

I'm also not a big believer in groundhogs being much good at predicting springtime. Groundhog day is February 2nd, and it is never springtime in Minnesota in February. I've only seen a few times when it has been spring in March. If I were going to check rodents for long-range weather forecasts I'd have to go with muskrats. In the spring of the year all the young muskrats are kicked out of their warm house and sent out into the world to find a place of their own to live. An unwary groundhog jerked out of his warm bed and shoved out into the sunlight doesn't mean much, but when a young muskrat starts measuring my garage to see if it will do for a townhouse, that's springtime!

As a farmer, I consider springtime my time of year. Easter means more to me than Christmas. It gets easier and easier to get out of bed. I find my days are much more productive and sometimes, when I am completely alone I even break into song. (It's not that I'm embarrassed to be caught singing, it is just a request my family has made.)

I have been farming for over 20 years now, and the whole spring process still amazes me. I love it when the geese and ducks start showing up. I find it incredible that a little shower of rain will somehow turn brown, dirty lawns green overnight. It makes me laugh when I see our tomcat who has been relaxing and getting fat all winter limping about scarred and battle-weary from defending his harem against the roving competition. I think he has reached the point in his life where the spring rush is not as much fun as it used to be but, like an aging champion, he is having a little trouble retiring from the game.

Despite all the years and all the acres, I am still caught up in the wonder and mystery of what happens when we take a little, dry, brown seed, put it in the ground, and a week later see a sprout of wheat. I know it is only warmth and moisture and time, just a lucky combination of factors that make life possible. It doesn't matter how well documented it is, it is still a miracle as far as I'm concerned. Think about it. Imagine someone trying to explain to you that if you would stick a little orange thing about the size of a woodtick in the ground, in five months or so you would have a plant eight feet tall and about 300 more of those same little orange things. I am still just a little surprised every spring when it works. It would be very difficult to be a farmer and not believe in God.

I think it is a mistake to make New Year's resolutions in January. Dark comes early and we are all fighting 50,000 years of evolution that makes us want to hunker down in front of the fire and eat lots of mammoth meat. There is so much time to think about your shortcomings in January and it seems to me that the more time you spend thinking about your sins, the more likely you are to repeat them.

I think we should make our resolutions in April. It is a lot easier to promise to do better when all around you there is an entire world in the process of waking up and transforming itself. Besides, who can concentrate on sin when there is corn to plant?

So, the thing of it is, is,

The one thing that I have a hard time explaining to people about farming is that everything is important. Let's say its springtime, and you've decided to plant a particular field to wheat. Let's say you're half done and you find out that old friends from out of town that you haven't seen in years are passing through and would like to take you to dinner. If you decide to quit early that night, you can probably finish the field in the morning. On the other hand, it might rain. Then it might rain again. You might not get back into the field for three weeks. The half-planted field would be grown up to weeds and you would probably have to plant the rest of it to soybeans.

Wheat is a crop that you plant as early in the spring as possible. You want it to be almost mature when the hard heat of summer hits, because if it is not, your yield will be cut severely. Soybeans can take the summer heat better, as long as they have moisture, and you can plant soybeans as late in the spring as you wish, just so they have time to mature before the first frost in the fall. Because you planted soybeans it will take you longer in the fall to harvest, running the risk of bad weather. Soybeans are harder to keep the weeds out of than wheat, and because you planted late the ground might freeze before you can dig the ground and turn the weed seeds under to rot. So there you are. One dinner out could cost you $5,000 in extra chemical costs two years from now.

On the other hand, maybe the price of beans will be very high, much higher than wheat, and you will by accident have made the perfect crop choice and pay for a whole year's college tuition for one of your children off one small piece of ground. You think this seems far-fetched? About 20 years ago my parents suffered a severe hailstorm early in the year. It wiped out all their crops. It was too late to do anything but replant everything to soybeans. That fall there was an early frost, which cut the soybean yields by a third. Things looked bleak because my father had just purchased a piece of land and badly needed a good crop to make the first payment. However, off the coast of Peru the anchovy fishing was particularly bad that year. There was an enormous shortage of fish meal, and manufacturers needed another source of protein and switched to soybean meal. The price of soybeans tripled and my father had all his bins full of soybeans. Not only did he make the first land payment, he paid off the mortgage in full.

You never know. Every day there are decisions to be made that have to be made right away. They will be right or they will be wrong, and usually there is no way to tell at the time. It is confusing, and exhilarating, and frustrating.

A neighbor and I purchased a no-till drill together. This is a fairly new invention for planting grain. It is designed to place seeds in ground that has not been prepared in any way. This saves on time and equipment costs and the theory is that over time there will be fewer weeds come up. The flaw is that there is very little margin for error and everything has to work just right. The drill has a disc, kind of like a sharp Frisbee, that cuts a slot in the ground. There is a tube that drops the seed into the slot. There is a little wheel that presses the seed down into the slot and there is another little wheel that runs at an angle and crumbles loose dirt over the slot and closes it up. Everything—the disc, and both little wheels—is adjustable. You can change how deep the slot is, how hard the little wheel presses the seed down and with how much force the slot is closed. If you make the slot too deep, the seeds can't force a shoot all the way to the surface. If you make it too shallow, the seeds won't have enough moisture to germinate. If you apply too much force to closing the little slot you form an instant pottery crust that seedlings can't penetrate.

Two years ago I planted the seeds fairly deep and we had three weeks of rain which packed the ground. Many of the seedlings couldn't force their way through and died. Seed that I just spilled on top of the ground had enough moisture to sprout and grow. Last year I planted more shallowly and everything worked fairly well. This year I planted at the same depth as last year. We had no rain, from April 3 until June 30 and about a third of the seed rotted in the ground. It wasn't moist enough to germinate the seed and wasn't dry enough to keep the seed from deteriorating.

Oops.

I wonder what I should do next year?

Hugging

I have some relatives who hug a lot. It isn't their fault, they're from California, but I still always find it disconcerting. I'm not a hugger. I don't know why. Maybe it's because I'm a pig farmer. Let's face it, a lot of the time I'm not real huggable.

Hugging is in style. Experts say that hugging is affirming and validating, along with some other words that people tend to use instead of words that actually mean something. They say that hugging is a way of saying, "I love you." They're right, of course, but there are other ways. Let me tell you a story.

This is a story about a wedding. The bride, who shall remain nameless because I didn't ask her if I could tell this story, has been married a long time. Like most people, I imagine, she remembers her wedding vividly, some parts more vividly than others. She was married in a little country church. The church was too small to have any sort of a dressing room for a bride, so she prepared at her parents' small farm home a few miles away. Like many houses in that era and in that part of the country, it was surrounded by a strong wire fence to keep the livestock away. Just as this woman was putting the final touches on her preparations, it began to rain. Not a gentle drizzle, but a real downpour. Our bride collapsed in a pool of tears. She had to walk 50 feet down an open sidewalk to the gate in the fence before she could get in her father's car to go to the church. All things are relative, and a 50-foot walk through a downpour by a bride who has just spent all day preparing for her wedding is a trip of some magnitude. Her hair, her dress, her makeup, it would all be ruined. Her father, like most men when confronted by a crying woman, did the manly thing. He left. The rest of the household huddled in shocked silence around the hysterical young woman.

A few minutes later our bride heard a horn honking. It was time to go to the church. She opened the door of the house and saw that her father had torn down the fence so he could drive the car right up to the house. He held an umbrella and she stepped quickly, one step only, from the house to the car.

I knew both the bride and her father. I don't know the relationship they had with each other, but they are of a generation that was more reserved than ours. It would not be out of the realm of possibility that there was never a physical expression of affection between them their whole lives. Did she know her father loved her?

"I love you" is perhaps our first and most basic message. You can say it with words. You can say it with a hug. Sometimes you can say it holding a crowbar and a pair of wire cutters, standing in the rain.

Diversity

I love living in a small town. It's so culturally diverse. I know you're thinking, "No, small towns are nice, but everyone there is just like everyone else."

You are so wrong. The fact that there are so few of us out here means we are thrown in with people that become our friends through sheer longevity.

I have a neighbor whom I consider a good friend who still thinks the commies are coming. He has a few other quirks but that is always the first one to come to mind. If we sat down and compared our philosophies, political and otherwise, I am confident we would not agree on much. I am also confident I could trust this man with my life. He is a wonderful man and my life would be a lot poorer if he weren't my friend. If there weren't fewer people in my county than in an average size apartment house I would never have bothered to get to know him. I would have found people just like me to know.

Have you ever noticed that a lot of people who like city life for its diversity tend to spend most of their time with people who look like them, act like them, and have the same kinds of jobs as they do?

There was an article in the newspaper not so long ago bemoaning the fact that there are so many wonderful young women out there who can't find a suitable husband. A woman was asked about what constituted a good husband. She listed the obvious virtues and then mentioned that she was really into sushi and any husband would have to share that same taste. Child, in my neck of the woods, if an affection for artfully arranged raw fish was a prerequisite for marriage, that lady would die a spinster. Around here if you hit a certain age without being married you stop looking for perfection and settle for a fixer-upper. This leads to occasional redemption through proximity. You can be the biggest jerk in the world but if your wife is a good woman people will cut you more slack because there must be some unnoticed virtue about you to justify her interest. I am always amused when behavior that would be condemned in an outsider is just brushed off as, "Oh, that's just the way Crazy Herman is. He didn't mean to burn it down. That Marge is a saint the way she puts up with him."

The next time you have visitors from the city and they talk about your lack of diversity, tell them about Ruth, the champion of the local Red Cross who just got her 12 gallon pin and is as mean as a rattlesnake. Explain that she single-handly made a whole county more careful, because no one wants to risk getting hurt, needing a transfusion and maybe getting a pint of Ruth pumped into their veins. Then mention that you are on a school committee with her and she'll be out for coffee in an hour. That'll teach them about diversity.

My Wife Left Me

My wife left me. Well, not really. She says she is coming back, but after 20 years of barely being out of arm's reach she was coerced into being a chaperone on a three-week choir tour of Europe. Coincidentally, the tour took place during the busiest spring planting season we've ever had. Since I am trying to be a good person, I sang only one verse and the chorus to "You Picked a Fine Time to Leave Me, Lucille" when I saw her off to the plane.

Being the sole proprietor of our farm is a new experience for me. I have jotted down a few household/farming hints. It was no bother. I did most of it while waiting for the rinse cycle to end at 1:00 AM.

1. If you are going to use the automatic bread machine, no matter how tired you are DO NOT substitute powdered sugar for flour. It will not make a quality loaf of bread. In fact, what it makes is a brown syrup that smells like yeast.

2. Never forget how many kids you have and that if you drop a child off at karate lessons, that child also needs a ride back home. This is important, because you do not want your mother-in-law telling amusing anecdotes to your wife that involve you calling her house wondering if one of the kids happened to be there.

3. Never wash your work clothes. What could possibly happen is you could put all your work clothes in the washer and then fall asleep on the couch before you put them in the dryer. That could put you in the position of doing chores the next morning wearing a swimsuit, black socks, and a Mickey Mouse tee shirt. This may be normal in your neighborhood, but it does occasion comment in mine. It is much safer just to wear dirty clothes.

4. Do not have public radio on in the tractor cab turned down low. A violin piece, played at the threshold of hearing, sounds exactly like a bearing going out. This can hamper production if you stop to find the bad bearing, and when you can't find it you drive up and down the field waiting for disaster to strike, until the violin piece ends and the news starts. Even this does not enable you to return to full production, because of the time wasted hitting yourself on the forehead.

5. If you are caught in a devastating rainstorm while you are out in the field, and if you are sitting snugly in the tractor cab drinking hot chocolate and congratulating yourself on not getting wet, of course the drill lids will blow open, and while you are lying on them trying to keep from having $600 worth of bean seed ruined, it will also start to hail. You know this is what will happen, so when it does, don't whine about it. It doesn't do any good and it makes your face wrinkle up.

6. If you are having trouble planning meals, just use the bread machine to make good homemade bread, then serve hot dogs at every meal. The wholesomeness of the homemade bread cancels out the turkey beaks and preservatives in the hot

dogs. This diet will sustain you for almost a month before scurvy sets in. Important! See item number one before using bread machine.

7. There is no need to do any housework while your wife is gone, as long as you keep careful track of when she is coming back, so you have time to shovel out the debris before she sees it.

8. When she comes back, you must walk a careful line between competence and eagerness to have her home. If you make the mistake of appearing not even to have missed her, you will be stuck with laundry and meals forever. On the other hand, if you have lost one of the children, wrecked the kitchen and forgotten to feed the cats for three weeks, you may never be let out of the hog house again. Good Luck!

Field Improvement Kit

About twenty years ago we had a grain drill that had markers that were activated by a rope fastened to the pivot wheels in front. The theory was that if you turned precisely enough, the pivot wheels would turn smoothly and pull one marker up while the other went down. The markers were exactly half the width of the drill and they would dig a small gouge in the dirt so when you turned around again you would have a nice clear mark to follow back to the other end. This helps you keep your rows straight which is very important. Grain grows just as well in crooked rows as straight, but the neighbors laugh at you if your rows aren't straight. Anyway, this concept worked well for a lot of people. Myself, I activated the markers by completing my turn, cursing, then leaping out of the tractor and flipping the marker down by hand. It wasn't all my fault. If there was a wind, and living as I do on the prairie there is always a wind, it would blow the rope back against the drill where it would catch on any number of protrusions.

One day the salesman stopped by and I jumped him about the problem. He got a roll of black electrician's tape out of my toolbox and wrapped about four feet of it around each end of the drill so the marker rope would hit the tape before it could get caught on anything. We tried it, and everything worked fine. I asked him what exactly I should call this modification. I still remember his words. "That," he said " is a field improvement kit."

What a concept! My life is always in need of a field improvement kit. I try to plan things carefully but it seems that at some point, no matter how carefully I have prepared, there is a need to drag out the roll of tape and cover up about four feet of bolts and sharp edges.

This is not necessarily a bad thing. If you think about it, most improvements in society are the result of field improvement kits of one kind or another. America itself is one continual field improvement kit. There are a few countries, Japan and Germany for example, that always seem to be working from some grand plan but not us. We just muddle along. What a talent that is! Anybody can work from a blueprint, but not everybody can make it up as they go along. There are even fewer who can take a blueprint, look at it, then throw it away. I imagine Mother Nature does this on purpose. Anyone who follows our political process will rapidly come to the conclusion that a building full of people all saying "Here, give it to me, I'll make it work!" is not necessarily a prescription for success.

As farmers, we don't tend to flock together nearly as much as politicians. This makes our tendency to use field improvement kits a little less dangerous, at least to the country as a whole. There seem to be a lot of nine-fingered farmers walking around, some of them I imagine as the result of a flawed field improvement kit.

That is the other side of it all. When you make it up as you go along, or meddle with the blueprint, it isn't always going to work out. That isn't a bad thing. It keeps the riffraff out of the field improvement kit business.

A lot of people won't try something if they know there is a price to pay. A thought for consideration is that if our leaders had to pay the price for their field improvement kits there might be a little more thought put into the product before it is field tested. That may be too much to ask, but hey, black electrician's tape won't fix everything.

Old Barn

There is the coolest barn not far from where I live. It is made of fieldstone, from floor to roofline. It is not that large a barn. In fact it is probably a little smaller than average, but it is the only stone barn I've ever seen. Most of the stone barns around here are only stone up about six feet high, about the height you could lift a big stone using simple equipment.

There is a square stone chimney in each of the four corners. They all open up on the inside at ground level. The theory is that the warm moist air would rise and pull dry air in from outside. I'm not sure if it works, but the theory is sound.

Unventilated barns are always either close and wet or dry and drafty. It was a very innovative way to naturally ventilate the building. That of course was a necessity because when this barn was built there was no electricity in the area for running fans.

When you go inside all the fixtures are made of concrete, and concrete of a quality of finish that you don't see anywhere, especially not in barns. Instead of a few boards nailed across wall studs to make a ladder up into the hayloft, there is a spiral concrete staircase. It is a staircase that would look good in a mansion, but you won't find one there because odds are you couldn't find anyone skillful enough to make one that looks this good. If you follow the spiral staircase up, you come to the haymow. This is, of course, a barn, and the feed and bedding for the animals has to be stored somewhere and that is what a haymow is for. It is unlike any other haymow you will ever see, because instead of a floor of creaking one-inch boards, this one has a poured concrete floor. There are no seams or cracks in this floor, something which is almost impossible. I don't know all the facts about how it came to be, and to tell the truth, I don't want to know. What I do know is interesting enough.

It was built long ago by a German stonemason who came to the prairie to farm. It took almost 20 years to build. I've often wondered why he built from stone when all around him neighbors were building barns from wood and having them ready to use in a month or less. Maybe his last job before leaving the old country was on a cathedral, and he was comfortable with starting a project that he might not see the end of. Maybe he wanted to leave something of permanence to his descendants.

There is, of course, the chance that he was just too damn stubborn and set in his ways to build any differently.

I talked once to the great-grandson of the man that built the barn. He told me a story that his father had told him, about helping on the barn. It seems that the old man had decided that his haymow floor would not only be of poured concrete, but it would be concrete with no seams or cracks. That is a highly unusual way to pour a floor. Usually you pour the floor a section at a time over a period of days, a process that leaves a series of seams. There are two reasons for this. One, temperature and humidity changes will stress a concrete floor and because of the low tensile strength of concrete this will usually cause it to crack. If you have a series of seams already built in, the concrete will quite often crack along those seams, called expansion joints, preserving the appearance of the floor. Two, it is a lot of damn work to pour concrete and there is a limit to how big a job most people want to do at one time.

The only way to pour a floor without seams is to do it as one continuous job. You start in one corner of the room and dump the concrete, level it off, smooth it, and finish it with a trowel as you go. Now this was all done back before there was such a thing as a Readimix truck on call. What they did have was a pile of sand, another one of portland cement and a pump. They had a long ramp from the ground up to the height of the haymow. They had a wheelbarrow, and they had an implacable old man holding a trowel who was good at his job and had decided that his barn was going to be perfect, no matter what it cost.

It isn't all that difficult to mix concrete by hand. You take about 10 shovels full of sand and two of cement. You can vary these proportions depending on how strong you want the concrete. You mix them together with the shovel and put a dimple in the top of the pile. You pour some water in the dimple and mix again, adding water until you get the correct consistency. Then you shovel the wet concrete into a wheelbarrow. If you fill it about half full you will be able to wheel it across level ground. I don't know how full you would fill it if you wanted to wheel it up a long ramp. Like I said, there is nothing difficult about mixing concrete by hand. The only problem is that it is an extraordinary amount of work. I've poured a lot of concrete in my life. Once for a week in Jamaica I even did it completely by hand. I know how much work it is, but I have no concept of what an exhausting enterprise that haymow floor was.

I often think of that old man standing impatiently on the form where the concrete will go. I think of his son, standing by the piles of cement and sand. I think of the teenage boy whose job it was to wheel the fresh concrete up the ramp. The guy who told me the story, well, it was his father who was the kid wheeling the concrete. His grandfather had told him that they were going to do this in one pour, without stopping, and knowing his grandfather, he believed him. The man had told his son that the single toughest thing he ever did in his life was push the first load of concrete up that ramp. They worked nonstop for 23 hours. When they were done the haymow floor was perfect, no seams, no cracks. It is still perfect 50 years later. Was it worth it? I don't know.

Hell of a barn though.

Buffalo Stampede

I'm afraid I don't understand how markets work. As best I can figure out, this is how the grain and livestock markets operate. It seems there are large rooms full of buffalo, called traders, and every now and then something no one else can see sets them off. They stampede around wildly, mooing loudly, buying and selling stuff that no one else buys, like pork bellies. Prices leap about, up and down for a while until the buffalo get tired and go back to grazing. There is no discernible sense or pattern to their stampedes, and people in the know tell me this is a good thing.

Among the things that affect markets are government reports. I think this is really funny, because I have been a source for some of these government reports. Some guy calls you up at 8:00 at night and asks you how much your corn is going to yield. First of all, it's June. I never have a clue how much my corn is going to yield until it is in the bin. Even then I'm not sure how many bushels an acre I got because I always forget whether you multiply or divide by eight tenths of a cubic foot to get bushels. Secondly, it is 8:00 at night. Even if I could come up with the right answer I wouldn't want to take the time because I'd rather get back to the Twins game. I usually just try to tell them what I think they want to hear and they write it down as if it were gospel. Thirdly, even if I did know my yields, why would I want to tell someone else? They'll just make it part of some report. When the report is published, the price of hogs will go down. Why should this make me happy? It's like playing poker with all your cards face up. I understand that the experts are asking the same questions of a lot more people than just me, but I fail to see how having 3,000 farmers lie to the government makes the report more accurate.

Another thing that cracks me up is the marketing advice given in farm magazines. If these people knew what they were talking about, they wouldn't be writing in farm magazines. They would be on the beach in Barbados drinking rum punch and watching someone count their money for them. Last fall one of these experts told me to sell everything I raised as soon as I could, because the prices were too good to pass up. Five months later the same guy gave me advice telling me to sell 25% of the grain I had left. Well excuse me! If I'd followed his advice, 25% of what I had in March would be nothing!

I think all of these marketing experts should have batting averages, just like baseball players. I know everyone complains about how much money professional athletes make, but their successes and failures are right out there for millions of people to see. If some of these advice givers had a little box score next to their smiling picture showing that in the last five years they have given the correct advice 37% of the time, it might cut down a little on some of their dumber tips. It certainly couldn't hurt.

Look out, I think another stampede is starting.

Life and Death

I was with some folks a while ago. City people, but not as dumb as some city people. That isn't a compliment or an insult. Just an observation. Anyway, at some point in the day one of them said, "What is that awful smell?" Without looking up, I replied "Something's dead."

I didn't elaborate, because it smelled like something sizable, a cow or a hog for instance, was dead and decomposing. I've always felt that short answers are better than long ones, and when possible it is good manners to spare people unpleasant information.

It was sometime later that I gave some thought to what an odd profession I have. I have an intimate connection with some amazingly disgusting things. You know, everyone talks about how neat it must be to be a farmer, because you have such a close connection to life. That is true. It is very difficult to be a farmer and not believe in rebirth and resurrection. The side of farming that people don't talk about much, is that you also have an equally strong connection to death. There is no help for it.

I can't grow an ear of corn without a seed dying first. And that is the least of it. There are about 3,000 hogs a year that get on the truck at my place and never come back. I have a firm grasp of the difference between people and animals, and I certainly do eat my share of meat, but when I think about this it does make me a little queasy. Not real queasy. In fact, when the occasion calls for it, I have done some butchering myself.

It still gives me a chuckle when I remember a college kid who worked for me one summer. There was a pig in the grower building with a belly rupture. It was still in good shape at about seventy pounds, but from past experience I knew it would never make it to market without dying of its ailment. I also knew that I wasn't going to pay a vet $300 for a hernia operation on a $100 pig. The kid thought it would be cool to have a hog roast/keg party at his house so I agreed to donate the pig. He thought it was a wonderful idea until we began the process that turned the pig into pork. It took about an hour from start to finish. By the time we were done I had the distinct impression that he would be going light on the pork and heavy on the beer at his party.

For my financial security, it is just as well grocery stores and slaughter plants bridge the gap between me and the consumer. I'm afraid pork consumption would drop if people weren't able to have the illusion that meat grows in those little plastic trays.

It wasn't always that way. I was an adult before we stopped butchering our own chickens and once a year a flock of relatives would descend on us for a day and we would take a couple of hundred chickens from feathers to food in a grim day of slaughter and plucking. Those days are gone and I sure don't regret it. I've done it, and if need be I could do it again, but God knows I didn't enjoy it.

There is a larger question here. I read somewhere in an article about the wonders of modern life that for the first time in the history of the world the average person does not know how the things that make up his everyday life work. I had a '66 Chevy pickup that you could take apart and fix with a screwdriver and a crescent wrench. Now I drive a new pickup and if it stops I tap on the gas gauge to make sure it isn't stuck, then I call the shop. The same thing applies to TVs and computers.

Is this the first time in the history of the world that the vast bulk of the population is sheltered from the realities of life, and death? People die all the time on TV and at the movies, but trust me, that experience bears little resemblance to butchering a chicken for the pot. We are sheltered to a large degree. Is it a bad thing? I doubt it. I am all in favor of painless dentistry and central heating On the other hand, I am very glad that I can butcher my own hog, and can face up to the fact that life and death are inextricably linked together, and everything that is alive is something that will someday die. Does that make me a better person than you, or just a more primitive model?

Who'll Stop The Rain?

It is raining again and I still have 300 acres of soybeans to plant.

Living as I do on the edge of the prairie, I have spent most of my life praying for rain. It is a hard habit to break, because I know that next week could see bright sunshine which will bake the ground to a hard crust, maybe followed by two months of no rain at all. It isn't likely, but I've seen it happen twice before in the 20 years I've been farming. In the cosmic scheme of things 20 years isn't that long, but this year it seems like I've been farming a very long time. In that 20 years I've lost two crops completely to drought, two to floods, and one to a truly spectacular hailstorm. There have been half a dozen short crops, and one failed thermostat that killed an entire nursery full of feeder pigs. There is nothing unusual about that. Talk to any farmer and he can recite a litany of bad luck, bad advice and bad decisions.

I am very lucky compared to many people. My family is all healthy and relatively happy, a state of affairs that you can take for granted. That hasn't always been a given. In a cemetery five miles from where I live are the graves of my great-grandparents, along with the graves of four of their children that did not survive infancy. Compared to that, my life is perfection itself.

I suppose the reason this year is getting to me is because it would be the fourth bad year in a row. I've got to do something profitable, sometime. It is the sort of thing that is expected of well-run businesses.

Like a lot of men, I pretty much define myself based on how well I take care of my family. In a book I read last week the hero found himself forced to protect his family from a rampaging grizzly bear while armed only with a homemade spear. Not a common occurrence, but stranger things have happened. My thoughts as I read that chapter were, "What a lucky stiff. All he has to do to take care of his family is fight a grizzly bear with a stick."

I've got to make it stop raining.

I Hate My Great-Grandparents

Now that the mosquitoes are hatching and hungry, I am thinking of my great-grandparents again. I hate my great-grandparents. Well, I don't actually hate them, but I am really disappointed in them. I know they have been dead for almost sixty years, but what were they thinking of?

Around 1880 my great-grandparents left Norway. We aren't exactly sure of the date, because they may have lied a little on their homestead application in order to qualify for some free land, but we know within a few years. They got on a boat and headed for America. I have no problem with their decision to that point. The thing is, boats go all over the world. Why on earth did they decide that the one place that would make them happy was western Minnesota? They could have landed in Florida, or New Orleans, or stayed on the boat and ended up homesteading near San Diego. Imagine what 160 acres of land in downtown San Diego would be worth now! I could be wearing nice clothes and negotiating rents with shopping malls.

The last time I spent much time thinking about my great-grandparents was in January. They were uppermost in my thoughts on one day in particular. It was a day when the visibility was somewhere between 30 feet and the end of your nose, the temperature was –20, and the wind-chill was about –90, but who's counting? I stumbled around doing chores most of the day, including a memorable hour engaged in fixing an outside feed system that had been designed for someplace else, like San Diego. I discovered that no matter how motivated you are, you cannot thread a quarter-inch nut while wearing mittens. I spent ten minutes on my knees in the snow, working on the feed system. When I tried to stand up, I couldn't. My coveralls had frozen into a frog-like crouch and I had to hop around until the ice limbered up enough to take actual steps. At this point, I paused to reflect upon those heroic arctic explorers who actually chose to live under conditions like this for weeks at a time. What kind of a twit would do something like this for fun! This was not fun. I've had fun, and it was nothing like this.

It was starting to get dark, and the wind had diminished to balmy zephyrs of about 35 mph when my father showed up and blew a path through the snowdrifts so I could get to our other farm to check the hogs there. I went to the farrowing house and was struck by the frozen door. This was nothing new; the door is frozen almost every day. Hog houses are full of animals. Animals breathe, that makes moisture. The best way to get the moisture out is to run an exhaust fan. The problem with that is along with the moisture you expel all that warmth that you used good propane to create. The temptation in the winter is to run the exhaust fans as slowly as possible to save heat. The correct ratio of moisture to heat seems to change every day, and that means doors stick with frost.

Unfortunately, a little frost wasn't the problem tonight. The door was frozen into ice six inches deep. This was a bit unusual. It turns out that there was a broken water line inside spraying water everywhere. The floor drain was plugged and so the water had run out under the door, until it froze. I got there when the entire building had about six inches of water in it. Luckily, the crates housing the pigs were all on stands eight inches high. None of the pigs were swimming yet, which was a good thing, because I'm not sure how long a hog can tread water. In addition, the water was very cold.

The reason it was cold was that the heater wasn't working. It took a little while to figure that out because the lights weren't working either. I found this out after about twenty minutes of chopping ice away from the door with an ax. Coincidentally the high winds of the day had broken one of the overhead electrical wires at about the same time the water line broke. There was electricity to only half the fuse box and it wasn't the half I needed.

It was now almost 8:00 PM. It had been dark for three hours and if anything it was colder and windier. I found myself in the bucket of a loader 12 feet in the air splicing wires. There was a certain added poignancy to the job since this was the last group of sows to use this particular building. I had decided to phase it out in order not to waste a lot of time doing continual maintenance on it. In two weeks it was to be empty forever. I toyed with the idea of seeing if the sows and pigs could make it for two weeks with no heat or water, but decided it would be poor stewardship. It was while I was up in the loader bucket that I discovered how much I hated my great-grandparents. As I write this, there is some guy sipping cafe latte or some other upper crust beverage, counting the revenue from land that should have been mine, if only Adolph and Marie would have had the sense to stay on the boat just a little while longer.

Love and Marriage

Our wedding anniversary was a while ago and at the supper table we were talking about what we first saw in each other. I told our kids a long, fairly touching story about how I noticed some of my bride-to-be's finer qualities at a party we attended for a group of developmentally disabled people. I expounded at some length on her sense of humor, her compassion, her gentleness, and several other virtues. The girls asked her what attracted her to me and she told them I smelled good when I picked her up on my motorcycle.

I dunno, I guess I was hoping there was something more.

It gets worse than that, because shortly after we were married I sold my motorcycle and became a pig farmer. For a marriage based on the sense of smell, that must have been a fairly shattering development.

As you can imagine, this was a disturbing conversation for me. Sure, we've been married for over twenty years, but what does that mean? She's probably just lulling me into a false sense of security then, bam, off she'll go with some fine-smelling stranger. I do know the plot to *The Bridges of Madison County*. I can't relax a minute without worrying about Clint Eastwood or some other "National Geographic" photographer coming through town.

On the other hand, maybe she made the whole thing up. Maybe she is just trying to keep me on my toes and is attacking me at my most vulnerable spot. If that is the case, she hit the nail on the head. As a pig farmer I'm sensitive about personal aromas. I never used to be, but after a few years of going to town, joining a conversation and having people sniff the air saying, "Whoa! What stinks? Is the sewage plant backed up again?" my spirit is pretty well broken.

Perhaps I am making too much of the entire conversation. When I met my wife we were both 18. I am now over 40 and it is sometimes hard for me to remember what was important to that 18-year-old. I look around at some of the marriages I see and it makes me think that I, despite all the evidence to the contrary, must have been pretty sharp at 18 because the choice I made has certainly paid off. On the other hand, I don't really remember putting a great deal of thought into it. If you do something brilliant for no better reason than that you can't help yourself, do you still get credit for being brilliant?

Marriage, at best, seems like an awfully haphazard thing. Ask the first half-dozen couples you meet on the street about how they met and how they decided to get married. The only people I've heard of who got married on purpose and with a master plan were Prince Charles and Lady Di. Look how that turned out. For the rest of us love and marriage is just something that happened. Pretty amazing when you think about it.

Keep Rowing

I read a book once about a guy who was a slave on a galley. You know—one of those ships with great big oars and people chained to benches. This was a pretty bleak life. Row all day, stop rowing to eat and sleep, then back to rowing. What the character in the book really hated was when the guy with the whip walked down the aisle and stuffed chunks of bread in the slaves mouths with the tip of a stick. This meant that they wouldn't be stopping to rest, but would just have to keep rowing until they collapsed.

Last Saturday I spent the whole day working around our yard. At about 6:00 PM I was looking around at all I had accomplished and started anticipating supper and a long hot shower. My wife brought me out a Coke and an Almond Joy.

Keep rowing, sucker.

I hope this doesn't make me a bad person, but I just don't get the concept behind yardwork. When we first moved to the farm we were so busy we just hacked a path through the weeds to our front door and called it good enough. No one seemed to mind, and the fact that we had burdock the size of redwoods in our grove was really no one else's business. We had to shave the dog every now and then when he started sticking to the furniture like a hunk of Velcro, but otherwise life was good.

Every year since then, we have pushed the wilderness back a little further. It must be the pioneer spirit that makes us do it. Our ancestors cleared this prairie and planted trees. One hundred years later we're whacking away at the groves they labored so hard to start. Is this progress? The first year we lived here we bought a lawnmower for $98 at the co-op. It cut a 17-inch swath, but only in short dry grass, and only for the first month that we owned it. Now we have a lawnmower that cost more than our first car, in fact more than our first two cars, and we still barely keep up.

I'm a farmer. I grow stuff for a living. I could have a nice yard if I wanted to. I just don't care. In my opinion, plants serve some kind of purpose. Wheat makes flour, corn feeds pigs and beans make tofu (although I can't imagine who actually eats the stuff.) I have no idea what purpose is served by growing acres of grass, all of it kept too short for anything to graze on. Flowers are kind of pretty, but wouldn't some rows of green beans be more practical?

From looking at all the manicured lawns around, I imagine my opinion is not one that is widely held, but think about it. If we all just bought a herd of goats to keep the weeds under control around the house, and if we remembered to shave the dog when he started sticking to the furniture, look at all the spare time we would have. If everybody did it, no one could criticize anyone else for crabgrass or dandelions. I don't need a decision from you now.

Just think about it.

My Neighbor Beats His Wife

My neighbor beats his wife. Maybe. I mean, I've never seen him strike her, but everyone says he does.

I don't know how to react. I find it hard to believe, but then, I am incredibly naive. I am always finding myself shocked at the secret behavior of people I know. What is my proper role? I am pretty sure that if I saw him about to strike her or one of their kids I would intervene, and on those rare occasions that I run into his wife I am extravagantly friendly, in hopes that if she ever feels the need to run she would feel free to run our way.

In my mind's eye I have cast myself in several heroic roles, but that is just in my mind's eye. The chances of me being in a position to thwart some dastardly attack are pretty remote. The problem I'm left with is that I don't know how to live day-to-day near a guy who may be mildly eccentric or who may be an absolute monster. Should I beat him up? Assuming I could, I'd be the one that would end up in jail. Should I shun him, tell him that I don't associate with people of his ilk? It would have been a little awkward giving him that speech last week when he was giving me a ride home after I had a flat tire on the road past his place.

I find this whole thing about domestic abuse confusing and utterly sad. I've been married for over 20 years and I have never had the urge to strike my wife. We've had some bitter fights, with hard feelings and cold looks on both sides, but hit her? Come on. If we men have a role on this planet, it is protecting the women and children. Any feminist reading this, please, don't yell at me. This isn't about women's rights. It is about men's responsibilities. I am completely in favor of women reaching their full potential, unfettered by discrimination. As a man with two sisters, a wife and two daughters, all of whom are smarter than me, I really do mean that. I fully support the right of any woman with the necessary character and judgment flaws to be President of the United States, or of the known universe for that matter. Having said that, I must add that if the President were walking towards me and she happened to be seven months pregnant and carrying a heavy briefcase, I would probably open the door for her. I don't think this makes me a bad person.

To get back to my point, the testosterone, the muscles, maybe even the hairy chest, all of it has only one purpose. Propagating the species? Study your biology. The human race only needs about 107 men to handle propagation. It is protection where we really are supposed to shine. "Women and children first" is not chivalry, it is a biological imperative. Men are the least important, most expendable part of society. This is not something unique just to humanity. If you look around, Mother Nature is fairly relaxed about the survival of the males of most species. We've got our assigned role, and once that's done, what happens to us is fairly unimportant.

It seems to me that in many ways our life is a search, an

effort to find something worth dying for. I'm fairly confident on this point, and a lot of the heavyweights in literature and in history seem to agree with me. Think of Henry V, at the siege of Harfleur. Shakespeare has him saying "Once more unto the breach, dear friends, once more; or close the wall up with our English dead!" Another example might be Horatius at the bridge, holding off the bad guys, "And how can man die better than facing fearful odds for the ashes of his fathers and the temples of his gods?" Not quite the ordinary conception of a pep talk, but it seemed to work.

Okay, I know that what Henry the V probably really said was "Let's get 'em, boys" and Horatius maybe never even really lived. That doesn't mean that Big Bill and Lord Macaulay were wrong. Anyone can write down the truth. A real artist can make something more than true, take an incident and show how it illustrates a basic truth beyond just the facts. If you are the "just the facts, ma'am" type, if you want an example that is probably a little more historically accurate, how about Crazy Horse at the Battle of Little Bighorn? There he was, relaxing around the teepee with his friends and family when all of a sudden soldiers came swooping down on the camp from three directions. He rode around until he had figured out the situation, then was faced with the problem of getting the warriors to follow him away from the immediate fight, so they could surround and neutralize the bigger threat, Custer himself, who was coming from the opposite direction. What incentives did he offer his men, to pull them away from safety? Legend has it he simply said, "Follow me, because today is a good day to die."

Most fathers will tell you that they are willing to give up their lives for their families. Very few of us are ever faced with having to put our money where our mouth is, there being very few lions or bears, or even General Custers left to slay. The most courageous thing most of us do for our families is put our shoes on in the morning and go off to work. Lord knows I am not trivializing this. Smiling and agreeing with the jerk who has the power to ruin your career can be an incredible act of heroism, especially when you are wearing wingtips a half size too small. The resultant stress can then make you act like a jerk to the very people whose welfare makes you put up with it all in the first place. The whole situation can make you think that the opposable thumb was a very bad idea.

We are all searching for something worth dying for. One of the most difficult problems of modern life is dealing with the fact that for a lot of us, the dying takes place a little at a time. That doesn't make it less heroic, just less noticeable. I'm not suggesting that we march grimly through life giving up everything for our families while reminding them of our continual sacrifices. There is nothing more boring than a martyr, and teaching your son that to be a man is to be a martyr is an enormous wrong. All I am saying is that being a husband and a father is the greatest joy and privilege to which a man can aspire and as with all joys and privileges there is sometimes a price to pay. If there comes a time when you have to pay that price, whether it involves dying a little or a lot, the most important thing to remember is when Crazy Horse was telling his warriors that today was a good day to die, he laughed.

A lot of things about our world puzzle me, but the current fascination with the idea of heaven tops the list. I don't know if there is a heaven. No one does. Still, if the idea of a life beyond your own is important to you, what in the world do you think children are? To draw your last breath, knowing that because you were alive there is at least one young person somewhere happier and more complete, is probably the closest you'll ever come to a state of grace.

So where does this leave me, with my neighbor who may be a creep? With apologies to John Donne, who shouldn't care since he is dead, any man's misdeeds diminish me, because I am a man and in a very real way the actions of other men are my responsibility. If he doesn't recognize himself here, no harm done. I've lived in small towns long enough to know that gossip quite often has no bearing on the truth. If he does recognize himself, let me make it as plain as possible. Neighbor, a man who harms his family is invalidating his very reason for being. A man who strikes a woman is contemptible. A man who harms a child is an abomination in the eyes of the Lord. Deal with it.

Mother's Day

Mother's Day. Big deal. Moms always get all the good press. I remember a few years ago around Mother's Day my kids were singing that mother song. You know, "M is for the many ways..." I asked, in a reasonable voice, why there wasn't a father song like that. They made one up right then and there. I can't remember all of it, just that "fat" and "hairy" were in two of the verses. It's lucky for them I'm broke, because if I had money, I sure wouldn't leave any of it to them.

I could go on for quite a while on how much better a deal mothers get than fathers. I could, but I am trying to be a good person so I won't. Instead, I thought I would pass on a few general parenting hints to any prospective mothers or fathers out there.

1. You will never, ever, get a complete night's sleep the rest of your life. By the time the kid stops waking you up crying for milk, you will be losing sleep wondering how they will do in school. Then you start staying awake waiting for them to get home, then after they leave home you lie awake worrying about what they are doing. After a while they get married and you can start worrying about jobs, grandchildren and global warming. It just goes on. You may live to a ripe old age, but if you have children, you're gonna die tired.

2. You will never, ever have any money again. As a general rule of thumb you can figure that children can spend as much money as you make, plus 10%. They can be vicious about it, too. Sometimes one will ask if they can take some money from my wallet. I'll say okay, and later in the day I will notice my wallet lying there, gaping and empty, looking for all the world like a gutted walleye.

3. No matter what you do, you'll be wrong. I've never quite understood how this works, but I know it's true. Sometimes, just as a test, I've argued both sides of an issue with my kids. I still lose.

4. No matter how carefully you plan, your children will not turn out the way you expect them to. I mean that, so don't make a lot of detailed plans for them. If you start saving money to send them to Harvard the day they're born, there is a very good chance when they're old enough they'll take that money, buy a used Camaro and join the Merchant Marine. If you've got your heart set on your child becoming a partner in your insurance agency, even getting little business cards printed for them to take to Head Start, they'll probably end up as ballet dancers in Atlanta. To avoid disappointment, don't make any plans for your children. When they come to you with some outrageous career choice, just smile and say, "Gosh, that sounds like a fascinating way to make a living." It won't do any good, but neither will anything else you can do.

5. If you decide to have children, take a deep breath and enjoy the journey. Being a parent is never relaxing, but it is never boring.

Father's Day

Father's Day was Sunday. Thanks for the cards and the tape, guys. I didn't get my dad anything. They don't sell cards at the fertilizer plant and that's the only place I've been the past two weeks. I hope he understands. I have a very good father. He's got a few minor flaws, but nothing I need to go into now.

All the ads on the radio lately have gotten me thinking about Fathers' Day, and being a father. I've been a father now for over 19 years. It has been, to say the least, an interesting experience. I just wish children would come with an owner's manual. I suppose a warranty is out of the question.

It hasn't always been fun. When they are little they can't tell you where it hurts and when they are bigger sometimes they won't. I've been dealing with other members of the human race my whole life, fairly successfully for the most part. I've been on a hospital board dealing with doctors and I've worked at schools dealing with teachers. Once I even got the IRS to agree that I was right and they were wrong. The only thing that can bring me to a state of lock-jawed frustration is a dispute with one of my children. The sad truth is that even when you can find out where it hurts, you can't always make it better.

Most of the time it's been really fun. The charm of playing a quick game of "Toes in the Nose" with a baby while you are changing a diaper is pretty much lost on most non-parents. Watching your child eating a dandelion out in right field and then actually catching a ball hit to him is wonderful, as is watching your child perform in a school play and having her remember most of her lines.

We were already living here on the prairie when our oldest child was about to be born. There was a chance there could be some complications so our doctor sent us to the Cities and the care of a specialist. Everything went the way it was supposed to and we had a son, in a place where we had no friends. Having a child is the sort of thing that you think the rest of the world wants to know about. In the little town where we live, most of the people do want to know. I was staying with my sister across town. Before and after visiting hours, I would drive around the metro area giving cigars to parking lot attendants and hitchhikers.

The morning after he was born I was sitting in the hospital coffee shop in a daze. I fell into conversation with an elderly gentleman sitting next to me. After I heard at some length about his wife's broken hip, he asked me why I was there. I told him that I had just become a father for the first time. He gave me a gentle smile that is still vivid in my memory. "Congratulations," he said. "The best time of your life has just begun."

I have three children now and there is seldom a day when I don't think about what that old man told me, and there is never a day that I don't agree with him.

Birdhouse

We live in a world full of mysteries. We live in a world full of miracles and unexplained happenings, and I have a birdhouse to prove it.

Well, not the birdhouse so much as what is growing out of it. There is this birdhouse, sitting on top of a ten-foot pole, and right in the middle of the roof an arrow sticks straight up. It looks like it came down with quite a bit of velocity. I would guess it went through all three floors of bird apartments. It must have caused no little excitement with the sparrows the day it hit. Just as a side note here, we didn't put up a birdhouse for the sparrows, we put one up for purple martins. We evidently live in a pretty low-rent neighborhood, because the only birds interested in our real estate are sparrows.

Anyway, about ten years ago I was walking across our yard and I noticed this arrow sticking out the top of the birdhouse. I have no idea how long it had been there. I don't routinely check the birdhouse roof for arrows, so it could have been there quite some time.

The really interesting part of this story is that no one on our farm knew how the arrow got there. It is probably just a coincidence, but we had purchased a bow and a bunch of arrows for the kids that summer. The arrow in the birdhouse looked a little like the arrows we had purchased, but who's to know for sure? Arrows look a lot alike. Besides, no one who was using the bow had any recollection of shooting an arrow into the birdhouse. Plus, the birdhouse is ten feet in the air. To get an arrow into the roof you would have to have been much higher than that. Unless, of course, you stood underneath the birdhouse and shot the arrow straight up into the air. Who would be silly enough to do that?

This birdhouse has always been a bother. When our son was very little he found a baby sparrow on the bround. He showed it to me and I said, "Huh, a baby sparrow. Well, he'll be dead soon." I thought that ended the discussion, but I soon found out otherwise. We have a picture of me teetering on the top rung of a ladder putting the baby sparrow back in the birdhouse. That wasn't even simple, because my son wanted me to make sure I was putting the bird back in the right apartment.

I found myself peering into the little doorways, looking for a family resemblance to the baby bird I had in my hand. It seemed to make sense at the time, but afterwards I wondered.

With this history in mind, I didn't want to start another birdhouse controversy. Everyone said they had not fired the arrow, and I was willing to leave it at that.

The theory we finally settled on was that a plane carrying a cargo of arrows going from Chicago to Seattle had an accident of some kind and at least one arrow fell out the door. This sort of thing hardly ever happens. Lucky no one was walking across the yard.

I left the arrow there, just so I'd have something to remind me that strange things happen sometimes, and it isn't always necessary that they make sense.

Getting Old

I drove to the Cities a while ago with my left turn signal on. I hate it when people do that. My children are amazed at what creative insults I can come up with when I am trapped behind some guy wandering down the road going 53 mph with his turn signal blinking. Not any more though. I've become one of them. I wasn't really planning for this to happen, at least not for a while. I'm still trying to decide what I want to be when I grow up.

I've never really been scared of getting old. I'm trying to prepare for it. Right now I'm trying to decide if when I get old

I will be like Mr. Rogers or Mr. Wilson from "Dennis the Menace." I could go either way. The little side effects of aging can be annoying though.

I've started to grow hair in my ears. This drives me crazy. Mother Nature, what is this, some kind of cruel joke? I need hair on the top of my head, not coming out the sides. What purpose does this serve? Would someone who got better grades in science than I did please explain what evolutionary imperative is satisfied by sprouting foliage in your ears when you hit middle age? I never gave it a lot of thought until I was getting my hair cut and the just-out-of-hair-cutter-school young lady got to my ears and said "Eww, gross." I didn't need to get charged $15 to hear that.

I don't feel as if I am getting older. Sure, it takes me 15 seconds to bend over to put my socks on in the morning, but I could do it faster if I wanted to. I just don't want to. My daughters hate it when I call them by each other's name, and they really hate it when I call them by the dog's name, but I don't think that is necessarily a sign of approaching old age. I do think about bran more than I did when I was 18. It is also a little disconcerting to realize that a professional athlete my age is either retired or just hanging on. It doesn't bother me a lot, because I'm not a professional athlete, I'm a farmer. In my chosen career I am just starting to feel like I'm beginning to know what I'm doing. There is a lot of room for improvement, and a lot of time to improve. I've been doing this for 20 years and if God, the bank, and my family are willing I could do it for another 30. I could last a lot longer than that.

I was talking to a semi-retired farmer the other day. He told me that he still goes out to the farm and drives tractor when they need him. He stays until he gets tired, and if something breaks, he just goes home. It seems like a much more fulfilling retirement than making a replica of the Empire State Building out of used toothpicks. There are times, such as when I've spent the day moving sows or cleaning out grain bins, that 30 years seems like a very long time, but by and large when the sun shines and the rain comes on schedule this isn't a bad way to spend your life.

Golf

I don't think just playing golf necessarily makes you a bad person. Everyone agrees that a real fondness for golf is an indication of a minor character flaw, but it doesn't mean that as a person you are beyond redemption.

It doesn't help, of course.

I've always been fond of Mark Twain's description of golf. He called it "a good walk spoiled." Sometimes when I am on an early morning mission in search of parts, I drive by a golf course. The air is fresh, the birds are singing and the few people strolling around the course look very happy. It does look really enjoyable. I sometimes think to myself that I need a hobby other than worrying about money, and golf looks as good as any. Later in the day I've driven by the same course. It will be 95 in the shade and the course will be full of people staggering around in the heat and humidity. This looks foolish to me. I can be hot and sweaty for free. It's even part of my job. Why in the world should I pay green fees and wear unflattering clothes for the privilege?

In my opinion there is only one way to combine golf and happiness. I've given this a lot of thought and it seems to me that this is the only way. The secret is to play golf three times a year. If you play three times a year, when you make a good shot you can gaze at it in satisfaction and strut a bit on your way back to the golf cart. If you hit a bad shot you just tell yourself, "So what, I only golf three times a year." All in all, you can't lose. It is about the fourth time you play that a change comes over you. You make a good shot and you say to yourself, "That was a great shot. You know, if I worked at this, I could get pretty good." At that moment your life is ruined and you don't even know it yet. Your enjoyment of the game is ended, your family is doomed to life without you around, and your world will soon be filled with frustration and aggravation.

I hope none of you golfers out there take this personally. I'm not trying to make you feel bad. It's probably not even your fault. Remember, golf comes from Scotland, a place where the men wear skirts and no underwear and in previous times used to settle disagreements with swords five feet long. Does this sound like a place that would produce a reasonable game?

To tell the truth, this isn't even my problem. It's not like I'm in any danger. I usually play only one round of golf each year, and that is in the winter at the Arctic Open on Lake Eli. I use a putter so I don't lose any balls and I still finish before dark. So go ahead, you people, live it up. I don't care. Fore!

Comfortable Clothes

I was talking to a guy the other day. He has one of those jobs where you pretty much have to live in a suit. He told me about the start of one of his weeks. It seems he had a three-day meeting scheduled in a town 200 miles away. He was about halfway there when he remembers thinking, "I feel so comfortable. There must be something wrong." He looked down and saw peeking out from the cuffs of his pinstriped suit, not the shiny wingtips he should be wearing, but instead the toes of the ratty old deck shoes he had worn to take the garbage out.

The story cracked me up. The thought that if you are comfortable on the way to work it must indicate that something's wrong is really funny to me. It is easy for me to laugh. There is no real dress code where I work No one notices how I dress, and if I am careful to scrape any lumps off my clothing when I leave the pig barn, no one cares.

It is probably just as well that I don't have to dress up on a routine basis, because I don't understand men's business clothes. First you wear a white shirt, guaranteed to show every tiny coffee spill and ketchup stain, then you cover up the shirt with a strip of cloth that you tie in a tight knot around your neck. On top of all that goes a jacket and then you go sit in a climate controlled office. People who know more about style than I do say that all this makes you look like a serious person. I don't understand that. No one thinks carpenters don't look like serious workers. If you were, for instance, an insurance agent, wouldn't you look just as serious if you wore jeans, a plaid work shirt and a big leather tool belt to hold your calculator and actuarial tables? You could have quick draw holsters for your stapler and white-out. When you called on your most important clients you could wear a vest full of pockets, like a SWAT team member. You could even Velcro your laptop computer to your chest for fast access.

I don't mean to make fun of only men's clothing. Have you ever really examined the concept of high heels? If this fashion were starting now, do you think it would catch on? "Here you go ladies, try this on. It makes you stand perpetually on tiptoe, it squishes your toes together until they turn upside down, and if you get the spike model you poke holes in linoleum every where you go. Added features at no extra cost—you can fall off them and sprain your ankle at any time and it is impossible to walk on ice with them." My personal opinion is that a nice pair of lace-up work boots would make you look just as serious and would be a lot more practical, especially if you wanted to hang some sheetrock on your lunch hour. We probably shouldn't even talk about nylons, let alone makeup.

This isn't my problem. After all, I am a farmer, I can wear whatever I choose. The deal I have struck with society is that I will toe the sartorial line for weddings and funerals and wear shoes in restaurants. Other than that society promises to leave me alone.

Works for me.

Churches

I was talking to someone the other day who was concerned about changing churches. She was afraid she wouldn't be accepted and would have trouble fitting in. She hoped the theology in her new church would match her old one close enough to avoid tension.

C'mon. If you volunteer to stay late and clean up after the fall festival, you can believe almost anything and get away with it. If you also volunteer to teach the junior high Sunday school class you could come to church in a black hooded gown wearing mirror sunglasses and the most anyone would say is "That Marge has a few quirks, but she sure is a good worker."

High school science teaches us that "a body at rest tends to stay at rest" but how many of us are taught that "in any volunteer organization there is 32% more work than there are people willing to do it." This is something I wish I would have learned in high school When you think about it, the two basic laws are kind of related.

You know the parable of the loaves and the fishes, where Jesus fed the multitudes with just some small fish and a couple of loaves of bread? I've often thought that the reason there was so little food around was because the people who were supposed to bring lunch had promised to do so and then remembered it was their bowling night so they just skipped it and hoped someone else would bring extra. Kind of makes the whole story hang together, doesn't it? Can't you just hear it?

"Say, how many came to that meeting the other night?"

"Oh, about a multitude."

"Huh. Well, I planned on bringing something but I was really busy. I hope you had enough food."

"Oh, we made out all right. Don't worry about it."

It can be frustrating living in a small town. There is so much that is worth doing, and there seems to be less money and fewer people to do it every year. If you were willing you could go to a meeting every night, and every meeting would be for a well-intentioned worthwhile cause. It is important to pick and choose. In our house, my wife and I try very hard not to go to meetings on the same night. I always felt it indicated a flawed system when parents are attending meetings promoting better parenting while their kids sit home alone.

On the other hand, there is a lot to do. Quite a bit of it is worth doing, and one of the blessings of living in a small town is that if what needs to be done isn't done, we have no one to blame but ourselves. One of my New Year's resolutions was to not give advice unless I was willing to carry out the plan, not just critique it. I haven't noticed much improvement in my community involvement, but I've cut way back on the advice I give.

So let's get to work. It's in our hands. Enough people live here to do the work, and there are few enough here so we can see the results. Is it my turn to bring lunch?

Women

I don't understand women. The sad part is that I really should. I mean, I have a mother, sisters, a wife and daughters. When I think about it, I spend more time around women than I do around men, but I'm afraid I just do not and probably never will understand them. I like women, but Lord, they can be confusing.

Take shopping for instance. This seems like such a simple, clear word. Why does it mean two different things, depending on whether a man says it or a woman? Let me run through a scenario, and see if you find anything at all familiar in it.

An important woman in your life wants you to go shopping with her. Obviously, she has to be important to you, otherwise you could never be persuaded to go along. This woman is looking for something simple, like a pair of black shoes or a dress for church.

This part is often the downfall of an inexperienced man. The woman will ask him if he wants to go shopping with her. He will make a face and then she will say, "All I'm looking for is a pair of black shoes." The inexperienced man will say to himself, "How long could that take? They have whole stores full of shoes in the mall. I could buy a pair of black shoes in ten minutes." The experienced man will set the VCR to tape he Vikings game since he knows he won't be home in time.

When you get to the mall you trudge through all three shoe stores looking for a pair of black pumps. I don't know why they are called pumps. When I think of pump I think of a piece of machinery that moves liquids from one place to another. I've never seen one that looks like a pair of shoes although sometimes the cost is equivalent.

Here is another place that sorts the men from the boys. If this is one of your first shopping experiences, when the woman holds up a pair of shoes and asks you how they look you will say "They look wonderful. I think you should get those." First, you should actually look at the shoes before you say this, and second, it doesn't matter what you think.

At some point during the day, if you are lucky, she will find a pair of shoes that she likes well enough to try on. This is the place where you will be tempted to say "How do they feel?" Don't. It will just show your ignorance.

Men have a lot of flaws. We scratch our bellies in public, a lot of us run for public office, and we have a tendency to start world wars, but at least we wear comfortable shoes. The concept behind shoes is here is an article of clothing that you wear on your feet to protect them from the elements. This seems like a great idea to me, and as a pig farmer it is one I and all my family really appreciate. So where did we go wrong? What's the deal with the pointy, spiky things that slip on the ice and get stuck in the mud?

If you are persistent, your shopping companion will find a pair of shoes that are the right color, the right style, the right size and the right price. She will try them on and they will look good and feel okay. You will be doing a little victory dance in the hall when she will put the shoes back on the rack and say to you, "Remember where we saw these. We'll come back here if we don't find something better."

Be strong.

Some Cats Run, Some Cats Don't

My daughter purchased a new puppy a while ago. It is a very nice dog, a golden retriever, but it is, you know, a pup. It has a few annoying habits, one of which is cat chasing. You can tell right away when the urge hits. Her ears prick up and her eyes get excited and then she's off across the yard. She's never actually caught a cat, but there have been a few close calls. The cats are getting damn sick of climbing trees and ducking under cars.

The other day I saw the pup light up and before I could say a word she tore across the yard after a cat. Dogs don't have particularly good eyesight. The pup didn't see the trouble she was about to get into until the cat was only about 15 feet away. Unlike the other cats, this one hadn't broken for cover but had continued to stump slowly across the yard, limping on one hind leg and with his tail dragging behind him. As soon as the pup recognized which cat it was, she slid to a halt, paused for a moment, then turned and walked slowly back to the house. The cat didn't even look up.

His name is BD. It stands for Black Diamond. He got it when he was a baby and still cute. He is no longer cute. He is covered with scars and welts, his tail looks like it has been broken and his life has pretty much narrowed down to food, sex, and beating the crap out of any tomcat that comes into his territory. He is getting older now, and every year he is in a little worse shape by the end of the spring rush. One of these years some wandering tough is going to catch him on an off day and beat him to death. I will be very sad when this happens, but I can think of no way to avoid it. "Do not go gentle into that good night...Rage, rage against the dying of the light." Dylan Thomas would have loved him.

One consolation is that the wandering tough that finally bests him will most likely be one of his progeny. He has several sons that hang around and take a whack at him every now and then. One of them was such a pretty cat that we had him neutered in hopes it would stave off combativeness. It didn't work. We now have a one-eyed, scar-tissued neutered cat who picks fights with his father and wishes he was still a tomcat. Sorry about that Ted. We had the best intentions.

I don't know why I am so fond of BD. I know people with the same personality and I don't like them. I certainly don't wish I were like him. I put a lot of work into being a role model. This beast wouldn't be a good role model for Attila the Hun.

Lord knows he isn't a very cuddly cat. He never really relaxes, always on edge to give battle, and has pretty much forgotten how to purr. If you pick him up his whole body tenses up, prepared for some trick. He can't be put down in the house because he does tomcat stuff at every opportunity. On certain rare occasions he will let you rub his belly and he'll tip over on his back and stretch his legs and wriggle his toes. After a few seconds of this he quite often shakes himself, leaps to his feet and bites you.

I think what I like is his inimitable—catness. If you watch Barry Sanders play football at some point you say to yourself, "Oh, so that's a running back." If you read an interview with Dr. Richard Feynman you say, "I see, so that's what a genius sounds like." If you hang around golden retrievers you realize that they are the essence of dogness. The Grand Tetons are the perfect mountains and the Taj Mahal is the perfect building.

BD, with his lack of charm and absence of a sense of responsibility or gratitude, with his scarred nose, bent ears and rumbling growl, with his twitching tail and combative eyes is one hell of a cat. I don't always like him, but I will certainly miss him when he's gone.

Car Accident

There are days when I wonder why I live in a small town. There is a certain amount of frustration and limitation that seems to go with small town life, and sometimes that really grates on me.

Sometimes, I remember why I live here.

Yesterday my wife was in a car accident. She wasn't badly hurt. A sprained ankle and a large assortment of cuts and bruises were the extent of her injuries. She couldn't move at all yesterday, but is a little better today.

It happened on a road a few miles from our house. The first people to the scene were a woman I used to work with and her husband. They tried to call me, and when I wasn't home they called my parents' house. This would hardly ever happen in a large city. I got there after the first responders, but before the ambulances. The man who was immobilizing my wife's leg is a janitor at the elementary school. When our children were small his wife was our day-care provider for a while. He had been holding her leg a long time. I had a desperate need to do something useful so I told him I'd take over. He said he was OK and then I said, "Mike, please, it's, like, my job." I don't know if what I was feeling showed in my voice but he looked up, nodded, and relinquished his spot. I knelt in front of my wife and tried as carefully as possible to hold her leg so as to minimize her pain, a job I've been performing with various degrees of success for almost a quarter of a century now.

The ambulance arrived and the first two members of the ambulance crew I saw were my daughter's English teacher and one of my former Sunday school students. At one point I looked up and there were about 20 people helping get all the injured sorted out. I knew every person there. For lack of a better word, there was an essential sweetness to the scene. Farmers in grimy work clothes and other people in their weekend shorts and T-shirts mingled in an atmosphere of concentration and concern.

I followed the ambulance to the hospital, but one of my daughters was working at the county fair so I thought I should stop on my way and tell her what had happened and that her mother was going to be okay. As I drove up to the fairgrounds I realized I didn't have my wallet with me, there was an admission charge to enter the fair, and our season pass was in a wrecked car being towed to a different town. I was trying to figure out the most efficient way to explain all this to the ticket taker. I rolled down my window and before I could open my mouth he waved me through and said, "How's Robin?"

That night after I got my wife settled uncomfortably on the couch, I went back to the fair to pick up some cheeseburgers with fried onions from the Methodist Food Stand. It is a family tradition that predates our marriage and is one of the essential tastes of summer for us. The cheeseburgers were cold before I made it home because everyone, literally everyone, I met needed some words of reassurance that everything was going to be OK, and offered a few word of sympathy. The obvious concern from our friends was cumulatively almost overwhelming for me.

One of my favorite quotes, and I apologize to those of you who have heard me say this too many times, is from Sam Rayburn, the former Speaker of the House. He was from a small town in Texas and after he was diagnosed with terminal cancer, he told everyone he was leaving Washington and going back home. His colleagues were aghast. Sam, they said, stay here. You'll get the best medical care in the world. Why go back to Bonham, Texas?

He replied, "Bonham is a place where people know it when you're sick, and where they care when you die."

I thank God that no one did die or was seriously injured yesterday, and right now I thank God that I live where I do.

Thank you all very much.

Cats and Rats

I bought cat food and rat poison yesterday. I feel this is kind of a sad commentary on the way I run my farm. This is what I believe environmentalists would call an ecosystem in collapse. It seems to me that the balance of nature would dictate that the cats would eat the mice, thus leaving me out of the whole process. It is certainly the way I would prefer it.

I have no real problem with mice in the wild. When I see them scurrying around in the field I even think they are mildly cute. Not real cute, no mouse I ever saw even vaguely resembled Mickey, let alone Minnie, but kind of cute. If they were to stay on their own turf, eating grass seeds and other mouse-type food we would get along splendidly. It is when they start moving into my turf that the animosity begins.

Mice drive me crazy. It is bad enough when they are in the house. We have an old house, and try as I may I cannot seem to close up all the mouse-sized openings. I used to feel this was a real failure on my part until I read that a mouse can squeeze through a hole the size of a pencil. This made me feel a little better, but also more discouraged, because the chances of me closing up all the openings pencil size and larger in our foundation are fairly slim. Every fall and spring we have a run of mice moving into the house. I trap them as fast as possible, disposing of the remains when everyone is at school, but we still go through a period of time when we find mouse droppings on the toaster. This causes a severe cutback in the amount of toast consumed in our house, at least until the toaster is cleaned, disinfected and then sterilized.

Rodents in the hog buildings are even worse. Not only are they just as annoying but they can cause real damage, way out of proportion to their size. It was a rodent in our farrowing house that gave me the worst scare of my life. One winter a family of rats got in my farrowing house. I really hate rats, and devoted my life to disposing of them. I trapped them, I poisoned them and every night after dark I would pick up my rifle, load it with birdshot, and tiptoe out to the barn and fling the lights on, hoping to catch one of wretches in the open. One night when I did this I quickly scanned the floor and saw nothing. I glanced up before leaving and saw, almost over my head, the shadow of an enormous rat on the wall. It looked to be about the size of a cocker spaniel. Since it was just a shadow it was difficult to judge intent, but I certainly felt like it was about to leap for my throat. The important word here is "shadow". I couldn't see the actual rat, just the shadow. I got my back to the wall, and with my heart pounding in my throat whipped my rifle in every direction. I was pretty sure my life was about to end but I was ready to go down fighting. My panicked gaze finally fell on a little, tiny mouse, tiptoeing along a water pipe about six inches away from a light bulb, and incidentally casting a huge shadow on the wall.

Now that I think about it, gosh I hate mice.

Alarm Clock

I got a lot done last Saturday. It's because I don't use an alarm clock.

My wife had an early meeting in St. Cloud on Saturday. This meant she had to get up at 4:00 AM. This meant she had to set the alarm clock. Now, I don't use an alarm clock. First, I pretty much wake up when I want to. Second, no one cares what I look like and I do only have an eight second commute to work, so I don't lose much time in transit. Third, I'm a farmer. I don't have a time clock. If I'm late for work, no one yells at me—I just go broke. These are all reasons why I was not expecting the alarm to go off Saturday morning. I suppose it has been a year or more since I've even heard our alarm clock.

I don't like it.

I was sound asleep when this horrendous noise shocked me awake. It sounded like an air raid siren. I didn't have a clue what it was. I thought the ship was sinking.

I flopped around in bed like a wounded carp, trying to figure out what was happening. I flailed away in the general direction of the alarm clock, but didn't hit anything useful. In the end my wife had to get up and run around the end of the bed and turn it off. She then went off to get dressed. I lay back down and closed my eyes. Unfortunately, my wife had hit the snooze button instead of the off switch.

That's right. Ten minutes later the cursed thing went off again. This time I turned the light on and figured out how it worked. When silence finally descended on the room, I lay back in bed and tried to catch my breath. My pulse was about 130 by then and relaxation seemed pretty much out of the question. I got up, got dressed, made a pot of coffee, drank it, and then planned the rest of my day. By now it was 4:30.

I know people who routinely get up at this time of day. This seems odd to me. I think of myself as a fairly open minded guy, but there is something a little unnatural, a little eerie about people who get up of their own free will long before daylight. People don't see very well in the dark, which leads me to believe that we are designed by nature to just curl up in the animal skins next to the fire and dream until it is fully light out. Don't get me wrong, I can get up early if I have to, but that doesn't necessarily mean anything. I can get a root canal when I have to. It doesn't mean I enjoy it.

Maybe the solution would be to work longer hours in the summer and shorten them as the days grew shorter. Come January and February about four hours a day would feel right. I'm sure there are other solutions that reasonable people could agree on.

I am just not convinced that the person who invented alarm clocks really had the best interests of mankind at heart.

Skunks

A skunk sprayed the bottom of the combine while I was harvesting wheat this year. I do not feel this is funny. My combine cab is not all that big. There is a limited number of variations of, "Man, that stinks!" that you can say to yourself as you trundle up and down the field basking in the aroma of a disturbed skunk. The day got really long, and no one would make a round with me.

I usually have a big thermos of coffee and sip on a cup off and on all day. For some reason, the coffee didn't taste nearly as good as it usually does.

It's funny how bright sunshine seemed to intensify the smell.

I did nothing to this skunk. I was just driving up and down my field providing for my family and gathering wheat to feed the world's hungry people. I was working in a field that my family has been paying taxes on for almost 120 years. I am sure it was a little startling for the skunk when the combine passed over his head, but if he had been alert he could have moved out of the way long before I got there. The combine is 20 feet wide, 12 feet high and incredibly noisy. It is the sort of thing that I would notice moving through my home.

Any of you who are animal rights activists, don't worry. I

didn't hurt the skunk. I saw him stalk away in disgust. At least, I saw his tail in the air as he made his way through the wheat into a slough.

The skunk reminded me of some people I know. They sit and loll around, relaxing, in someone else's way. Then suddenly there is an uproar caused by people trying to get something done. This disturbs their rest and they leap to their feet, spraying foulness in all directions.

What is so destructive is that it doesn't take much foulness to bring progress to a halt. Have you ever been in a meeting where someone comes up with a brand new idea? Someone else takes the idea and expands on it. A couple of other people grasp the concept and add their suggestions. Things will be humming along nicely until one member of the group says, "That will never work." The skunk in the group will list a few reasons why it won't work and everyone will settle back in their seats, enthusiasm gone and all momentum halted.

Of course, it is important that we should have a certain amount of caution about new ideas. The thing is, it is easy to find reasons why a new idea won't work. It was easy for people to give Henry Ford reasons why he couldn't make a living making automobiles. It must have been very easy to tell the Wright brothers that they would never get their airplane off the ground. You can even make a pretty good case that it is impossible for a bumblebee to fly.

That doesn't stop the bumblebee. Don't let it stop you.

Christianity Test

I flunked my Christianity test last week. It wasn't fair. I didn't even know I was being tested until after it was over, but too late. I'm sure I flunked. And all because of a box of popcorn.

You see, there is a certain public etiquette in eating a box of popcorn. If you are standing in a public place and an acquaintance comes up to you and starts a conversation, the acceptable thing for you to do is to tip the box of popcorn in their direction and raise one eyebrow in a questioning manner. At that point the person talking to you either shakes his/her head slightly and keeps talking, or reaches in and takes a few token kernels. Doesn't sound too tough, does it? Certainly doesn't sound like any kind of a test.

Here's what happened. I was standing by my pickup in town eating a box of popcorn when this guy I know came up to me and started to talk. I didn't offer him any popcorn.

I'm not even sure why I didn't. I didn't even think of it until after he left. His fingers were a little dirty, but that is certainly no reason for me to feel superior. Most of the people I know spend the day with dirty fingers. Plus, I've been a pig farmer for 20 years. You don't want to know some of the places my hands have been. When I stop to think about it, there aren't many people who take popcorn when I do offer it.

This would not have bothered me nearly as much if it hadn't been a Monday morning, after a Sunday in which the reading had been that quote "As you have done it to these the least of my brethren, you have done it to me." Wonderful. I hadn't offered the Big Guy any popcorn. This couldn't be good.

By Tuesday I would have forgotten the lesson. I've found that a faulty memory and an elastic conscience are the keys to the painless practice of Christianity.

So here I am, feeling guilty because I didn't offer this guy some popcorn. I don't quite know how to fix it. I've been spending a lot of time in town lately, hoping I see this guy and he's eating popcorn. With luck, he won't offer me any. It would make me feel so much better.

Concrete Igloo

If I ever build a house, it is going to be a concrete igloo in the middle of an asphalt parking lot. It won't have any windows to wash or shingles to blow off. It won't have a basement to get wet and it won't have any eave troughs to plug up. If I can arrange it, I'll build it under a waterfall so I won't need to install plumbing. I would even consider building over a volcano so we wouldn't need a furnace.

We live in an old house. When we first moved to the prairie, 20-some years ago, we decided that we would fix up the house one room at a time as we could afford it. Now the first rooms we did are worn out and need to be redone. And we have two rooms we haven't yet done! This seems like a really bad omen to me. The only thing that has sustained me through 20 years of remodeling is the hope that someday we would be done. I don't know what purgatory will be like, but I am pretty sure that Sheetrock dust will be involved somehow.

Don't get me wrong. There is an upside to living in a never-ending construction project. Number one, I've lived a fairly moral life the past 20 years because I've always been too tired and too poor to pursue any of the more interesting bad habits. Number two, if you are missing walls and ceilings you never actually need to clean anything else. If someone stops by, instead of scurrying around spiffing up the house you can just show them in and say, "Excuse the mess, we're remodeling." When you use this phrase, people will nod in sympathy and never question what dirty clothes under the dining room table have to do with painting the bathroom. Number three, remodeling your home brings the whole family closer together. At times our family has grown so much closer we can read each others minds and tell exactly what the other person is thinking. On the other hand, mind reading is not an unmixed blessing.

I think the worst part about remodeling your house a bit at a time is that it takes so long. Tastes do change. We moved here in 1976. Our first doorbell was a tiny Chinese gong. We used to have wallpaper with great big purple and green flowers on it. Since you're always saving money to do the next room, you can never afford to fix the ugly thing you did five years ago. For many years we had one room in our house that was hidden from the public. If we ever would have had a fire at our house while we had company, and the only way to safety was through that room, we all would have had to burn to death. No one was going to see that room. It's all fixed up now, but what it used to look like is still pretty much a secret.

Sometimes I really like our old house. My great-grandparents did build it and it is really neat to feel that connection to my past. On the other hand, there are days when I would trade all my ancestral connections for one square wall, one level floor and a drain that didn't plug up.

The other day I climbed up on the roof to change the TV antenna. I think the house needs shingling.

Cucumber Season

Cucumber season opened yesterday. I hope you got some good ones at your place. We have an opening day ritual here on the prairie. It is fairly simple. All you need is a box of shotgun shells, two participants (one shooter and one chucker), and a cucumber patch full of old yellow cucumbers. The chucker takes a cucumber and throws it straight up, while the shooter sets the 12-gauge on "puree" and lets fly. With number six shot at a range of about 20 feet, the results can be spectacular. One of the great benefits of living on a farm is that you can do things like stand in the garden with your son and slaughter vegetables without witnesses. If we lived in town I can't help but think that this sort of activity would occasion comment.

It is a fairly relaxed sport. If you get in a zone and with your first shot blow a cucumber in half, and then disintegrate the largest remaining piece before it hits the ground the chucker can, at his option, say, "Good shooting, Tex." If you miss completely, gentle ridicule is acceptable, but harsh needling is considered bad form.

As far as sports go, it is fairly silly, although it does not approach America's Cup racing or presidential elections in terms of sheer uselessness. At least we are making mulch.

I was pleased when my son came and got me out of my office with the news that, in his mother's opinion, cucumber season was open. It has been an edgy year for us. Bad weather on the farm for the fourth year in a row, money shortages, and his turning 18 and graduating from high school have all combined for an extensive run of raw nerve endings. When he opened the door and asked if I had time to stalk a few cucumbers, my heart lifted in a way it hasn't for a while.

I was impressed with his courage. We had been tiptoeing around each other for a while, each trying to maintain his own position, but trying to avoid making some irrevocable statement. I was quietly frantic that he make good decisions about his immediate future and he was just as quietly determined that the decisions, whether they be bad or good, would be his. I felt that I had been walking a tightrope for quite a while, trying to give him good advice and hoping he would take it, while the faces of all the grown men I knew who had never stopped listening to their daddies, and how pathetic they were, kept flashing before my eyes. He had been walking the same tightrope, between wishing his parents would just tell him what to do, and wishing I would leave him alone and stop having earnest chats with him.

He is our oldest child, and this is all new to me. I try to remember what it was like to be his age. That should help, but he is not the same person I was, and these are not the same times.

I don't know a great deal about therapy. I have had neither the time nor the money for it, although a majority of my friends and family are on record as suggesting that it would be a good idea. From what I have read, very few responsible therapists recommend going out in a garden with a firearm and the person who is making you crazy. It seems to work for us.

He had enrolled in a school and applied for and gotten a music and drama scholarship. He was relieved that he had something to tell people when they asked what he was going to do after high school, but I could tell the decision didn't light him up. A month after his application for college had been accepted, he told us that a Marine Corps recruiter was coming.

I wasn't sure how to react. My family covers the range from Quaker to Colonel with everything in between. I wanted my son happy; but I also wanted him safe. The bottom line was that even if I could have decided what I wanted, it didn't make any difference. It is his life, and that is how it should be.

There had been a few other tensions between us. Some

were my fault and some were his fault and some were nobody's fault.

I have a quote on my desk from some eminent somebody that reads "When you see God face to face, he's not going to hold you accountable for the entire world. But he will hold you accountable for what was entrusted to you." That quote weighs heavy on my shoulders some days, but I'm feeling much better now.

It's cucumber season again.

Pickup

We've got this pickup on our farm. It belongs to my son. It was purchased new in 1966 by my great-uncle. I purchased it from his estate in 1978 for $400. In 1994 my son got it from me and put a $600 stereo in it. Times change.

It's been hanging around our farm while he's been awaiting orders to where he will be stationed. He called a while ago from Georgia and said he'll be in California for three years. It'd be good for him to have wheels while he is there so we talked a bit and decided he should take the old pickup. It's in good shape, except for the fact that it screams and howls whenever you go faster than 54. This is, of course, an unacceptable level of speed so I was delegated to explore various go-faster options.

Like a lot of things in life, this seemed like a fairly simple task. I thought I would call a couple of mechanics, they would tell me whether or not there was anything that could be done, give me a couple of estimates and we would go from there. I should know better.

The first guy I talked to told me to put a new engine and transmission in it. Coincidentally, he had an engine and transmission for sale. The next guy told me to put in a new rear end. Number three told me to keep the old rear end and put new gears in it. Number four told me to keep the engine and rear end, but put an overdrive transmission in. Number five told me to just tell the kid to drive 50 mph and number six told me to bring the truck over and for $25,000 he would turn it into an award winning street rod.

I was beginning to get a bad feeling about all this. I had made six phone calls and gotten six different recommendations, with a price range of $0.00 to $25,000. I try not even to change spark plugs if I can help it, and I was beginning to feel like I was in over my head. I swallowed two aspirin and a Tums and took the rest of the day off, doing dumb stuff like try to run my business.

I made a plan, the way I make most of my plans, by lying awake at night and thinking bad thoughts about whatever ancestor of mine climbed down from the trees and began to evolve. In the morning I called three different parts suppliers about going with option number four. All three said I could do that, but it would be stupid, instead I should go with option two. They all said it would be cheaper, faster, and better. So much for my intuition.

We decided to go with option two and it looks like it might work. In the meantime my son found out that his pickup won't pass the emission control tests to be registered in California, so he bought a car.

When I get old enough to go into a nursing home I want to be wheeled into the sunshine every week, and I want the fresh Jello. I've earned it.

Shingling

My wife and I know someone married to a worthless husband.

So my daughters and I shingled our house.

Stay with me on this. It does make sense. There's this couple
we vaguely know. He is basically useless, and she basically puts
up with it. Several times a year we get updated on their domestic situation through the grapevine. It is usually confusing,
because she is always kicking him out for being useless, then
later he says he's sorry and performs some small service, like
changing the oil in the car or shoveling the sidewalk and she

lets him come back. Every little shift in their relationship used to make me angry, but the last few years I've just sort of shrugged my shoulders and tried not to think about it. It's frustrating to watch, but not really my problems.

Lately though, I've been thinking about it more. I have two daughters. One of the pleasures and pains of parenthood is thinking about your children's future. I decided that I was going to do whatever I could to make sure that neither of my daughters would put up with someone worthless just because he shoveled the walk or changed the oil in the car.

Coincidentally, our house needed shingling.

Now, we have a big house. Two stories high, with a dormer and three porches, one of which has five sides. It is like a graduate level course in shingling. It came to me that if my two daughters and I could shingle our house and not have the roof leak and not get hurt, and if after it was done we would all still be on speaking terms, there should be a definite life's lesson here.

Everyone I discussed this with thought I was nuts. They didn't all tell me that, but that certainly was the impression I got. I was unmoved. My daughters were willing, but dubious.

I was a little scared though. It is a big house, about 30 feet to the ground, which is plenty high enough to get badly hurt. I knew that if either of the girls fell my only hope would be to jump off the roof and hope I beat them to the ground. With my father's help we made a set of scaffolding that could have been a pin-up picture in the OSHA locker room.

I procrastinated for a couple days, then one day I woke the

girls up early, took a deep breath, and climbed up on the roof with them and started pulling the old shingles off. We worked in fairly easy stages, because I was afraid of taking too many shingles off and getting rain before we could get the new ones on. I did miscalculate one day and we had to work with flashlights as mosquitoes hovered around our heads and lightning flickered on the horizon.

Our skills improved rapidly as we progressed. We shingled as much the third day as we had done the entire previous two days. My daughters are possibly the only kids in their respective classes who know how to load a pneumatic nail gun. It took us about a week to do the whole house. We finished with a flourish, took a few pictures and cleaned up the mess. All the blisters have healed by now and the cuts are just fading scars.

We had a bad storm last night, over an inch and a half of rain. The roof didn't leak and my daughters know they can do anything.

Life is good.

Teachers Conferences

We had parents/teacher conferences a while ago. I don't know how it's done where you live, but at our daughter's high school all the teachers drag tables into the gym and set up shop around the edge. The parents mill around in the center like a herd of steers preparing to stampede, trying to guess which teacher will be free next. It can be a frustrating experience. I once talked to a teacher for five minutes before we remembered he didn't have any of my children.

Things usually start out pretty smoothly. If you get there early you can pretty much have your choice of teachers, and the teachers are still fairly fresh and ready to give you an honest opinion, or at least as honest as they think you can stand. Later in the night the place fills up with grim parents trying to get teachers to explain why they are so unfair to their darling child, and the teachers get a little worn down from saying, "I just don't think Billy (or Suzy, or young Fleming) is working up to his/her potential."

I used to think that conferences would be a lot more productive if all parties felt free to just tell the truth, without worrying about hurt feelings. Teachers could say, in a nurturing manner, "Your son is lazy as a dog and dumb as a rock. He is further handicapped by having two of the worst role models since Adolph Hitler and Eva Braun, namely you and your lovely wife."

Parents in turn could say, "I think I hear where you are coming from, but I can't help but think that part of the problem is that you haven't taken your job seriously since 1975, and have devoted your life to a crusade for decent coffee in the faculty lounge."

Sounds like a nightmare to me. The older I grow, the more I come to believe that the basis of civilization is the polite lie.

I was talking to a group of parents at the last conference we attended. As a group we had followed this routine for many years. We came up with what we thought was a great idea.

Wouldn't it be a nice touch if the year your youngest child was a senior, the school would come to your house for conferences? You and your spouse could sit on the couch in the living room, and all the teachers could sit on hard chairs out in the hall, next to the coat closet. They could wait out there until you summoned them in.

I mentioned this idea to one of the teachers, and he had an entirely different outlook. Oh, he thought it was a great idea, but for a whole different set of reasons. He said, and I found this shocking, that teachers don't enjoy conferences all that much either. Most families aren't much bother, and some are even enjoyable. The trouble comes when you do hit a bad one. As a teacher you work your way painfully through the conference, trying to be tactful while your skills, dedication, and sometimes your ancestry are being maligned. After it is over, you lean back in your chair and a mental picture of all the kids in this family forms in your mind, stretching back to a babe in arms. With a little luck, you will be going through this same painful experience, with this same family, every year your entire career. My teacher friend said that when the last child from one of those families became a senior, he would be glad to come to the house for the final conference.

He'd even bring the champagne and little crackers.

Fall

Fall is what you wait for. Fall is harvest time and the whole year points towards it. There is a rush and emotion to it that is hard to describe. There are very few jobs that make you work all year just to give yourself one chance to collect a paycheck.

Typically soybeans ripen before the corn does. That is good because soybeans are harder to harvest than corn and require better conditions. The soybean pods cover the plant, right down to ground level. The best way to harvest them is to use a floating cutterbar, a long flexible piece of metal with sharp teeth on it that are pulled rapidly back and forth. This rests lightly and directly on the ground. As you drive along, the cutterbar cuts the soybeans off and the reel, a big circular thing that looks like the paddlewheel on a steamboat, pulls the beans into the combine for processing. If the ground is wet is doesn't work well because mud builds up under the cutterbar. If the ground is rocky it doesn't work well because you have to worry about rocks getting pulled into the combine. If the field is weedy it doesn't work well because the weeds are usually more moist and can plug the combine. Corn on the other hand is relatively easy to harvest. The ears of corn are three or four feet in the air and you use a different attachment to the combine that just pulls the ears off. You can harvest corn in practically any kind of weather that permits you to get into the field. The only exception is when there is a lot of snow on the corn stalks. When that happens some of the snow gets into the innards of the combine and is melted by the friction in the threshing portion of the combine, then it freezes when it reaches the separating portion of the combine and plugs everything up.

The hours can be incredible during harvest. You are usually racing to beat winter. Humidity is lower than in the summer and most combines have from 6 to10 headlights so your work can extend about as far into the night as you are willing to go. Eighty hours a week is normal and one hundred hours a week is not uncommon. Huge machinery goes past your house at all hours of the day and night. Twenty years ago most people farmed the land close to where they lived, but as more and more farmers retire or go under the average farm has become spread out. Now many farmers drive for twenty miles or more to farm. If you stand in the darkness and quiet away from your building site you can hear machinery and see lights working the land in every direction. The crisp air of fall without humidity or pollen lends an extra sense of clarity to what you are seeing. A combine's headlights are not like a car's, but instead angle down sharply in order to provide near perfect illumination in every direction within about twenty feet of the combine. There is usually an enormous dust cloud created by the threshing process and the light reflects off it. At night, when the air is still, combines lumber up and down the field, each appearing to float in its own little bubble of soft light.

Once the crop is harvested the pace continues. An old

farmer saying is "The worst job of tillage done in the fall is better than the best job done in the spring." That means if you can open the ground up in the fall, the rain will soak in and the normal freezing and thawing cycle will mellow the ground. If the ground is not opened up, much of that rain will run off, and in the spring you will have to lose valuable moisture by working the ground then and exposing it to the harsh winds of spring. The old saying isn't always true, but it is true enough, so as soon as the harvest is over there is a big push to get all the ground worked. If you get all the ground worked, then there is a big push to get ditches cleared out, trees trimmed, grass cut short so it won't catch snow. In an average year there is more work to be done than can be done so the race continues until inclement weather shuts things down for good. The first real snow of winter is quite often welcome for if it did not come we could not rest.

Caution—No Stomach Scratching In This Area!

I almost died yesterday, from not tucking in my shirt. Wouldn't that look awful in an obituary? Man, 40, dies from farm accident caused by scratching his stomach while combining corn.

I am really a pretty careful guy. There was that time I shot myself in the hand with a rifle (don't ask) but by and large I am very careful. All our power takeoffs have shields. I never take chances when pumping the hog pits. I even wear my seatbelt most of the time. It never occurred to me before that I have to be careful about my wardrobe, too.

One of the big benefits of being a farmer for me is not worrying about what I am wearing. I wear OshKosh jeans, the ones with the hammer loop and the pliers pocket, because they are baggy enough so I can gain quite a bit of weight before I have to buy a larger size. That has always been my main clothing priority. My shirts are a mixed bag of workshirts bought on sale and good shirts that my wife has removed from public viewing. There is one shirt that I have been quite partial to. I don't know where it came from, but it is enormous, it comes down almost to my knees. It is just the ticket for wearing when the cold winds begin to blow. Securely tucked in, it really helps to avoid that frozen kidney feeling you can get from stretching to reach a bolt on the north side of a combine in the first week of November. Its only flaw is that when it is securely tucked in, you just can't scratch your stomach.

Anyway, there I was, combining corn wearing my warm shirt, with my stomach freshly itched, when I heard a strange sound. Everyone knows how welcome a strange sound is when you are combining. It turns out that it was a broken flight on a raddle chain, but I didn't know that. I flipped open the shields so I could see where the sound was coming from. I was standing on tiptoe when for some reason I looked down and saw my favorite shirt flapping in the breeze about a half inch away from the cylinder drive belt.

I have always known that I am engaged in the most hazardous occupation in America. We flip-flop back and forth with coal miners, but farming is always in the top two. More dangerous than construction work and as for being an undercover cop? Sorry, Serpico, I wouldn't want to do your job, but of the two of us, you have a much better chance of finishing your career alive and with all your appendages still attached.

My wife gets really tired of me coming in with bruises or cuts. Just last month I was headed towards my folks' house, holding a cut shut when my son came running up with a greasy rag. He said, "Wrap this around your hand. Grandma hates it when you bleed on her floor." I'm sorry, but everything I work around is big, heavy or moving fast.

So far I have been lucky. Nothing cut off, no permanent disability, just a few scars. The truth is though, it has been luck that has kept me safe. I have enough life insurance to keep a Rockefeller afloat and I try to keep my affairs pretty much in order. On the other hand, it may be conceit on my part, but I really think my family would miss me if I were gone.

I read somewhere once that an astronaut was just a guy who never has made a mistake when it mattered. Is that what I have to be, someone who never makes a mistake? I'm not sure that I'm up to that.

Remember the TV show "Hill Street Blues"? Remember when the crusty sergeant would admonish the cops right before they hit the streets? "Be careful out there," he would say, every day. Farming is a lot more dangerous than being a cop. Who is going to tell us?

You can't make foolproof machinery. My auger has a screen over it so I don't stick my hand in it. The only problem is that the screen gets plugged with soybean pods so you have to shut the auger off and clean it out. Am I going to shut if off every time, or once will I just reach down to flick the pods off and lose my hand? Will the auger company then have to put a smaller screen on their augers? It'll plug up faster. Truck drivers have to keep log books and when they have put in their time they are forced to pull over and sleep. Airline pilots can only fly for eight hours at a time. How many farmers quit after eight hours? The truth is, we quite often work alone. We work with dangerous equipment, under adverse conditions, when we are tired and stressed out. That's not going to change.

Be careful out there.

Duck Hunting

I like hunting ducks. I don't know why. It is such a difficult sport to explain. You get up early, pray for bad weather, wear uncomfortable clothes made of canvas and rubber, wade through muck up to your waist carrying a gun that weighs about 10 pounds, and then blast away at pretty little feathered creatures that don't even taste that good. If you wanted a good meal you could sneak up on a flock of leghorns. In the cosmic scheme of things, it's a dumber sport than even golf.

I like it though.

I'm not as fond of the actual killing as I used to be. It would be great if you could hunt ducks with a paintball gun. Then if you hit one, he could circle around, land in your boat, you could shake hands, and he'd say, "Helluva shot, champ!" Then he could buy a round of beer and fly off to join the rest of the flock. Now that would be a sport.

Another alternative that would make it a little more interesting would be if the ducks would all carry little tiny bombs on their feet they could drop on duck hunters. That would certainly liven up the hunt. It would also keep some of the riffraff out of the sport.

I have a friend who is a really good duck hunter. His camouflage outfit matches, his duck call sounds like a duck, I think he even cleans his gun. We're talking a real fanatic here. I took him duck hunting not so long ago. The way he usually hunts is to scout the terrain, study the habits of the indigenous duck population, arrive at his chosen spot before dawn, carefully place his decoys in an inverted fishhook pattern, (a known duck attractor), and disperse his hunting party carefully in the concealing cattails. Once everyone is correctly placed, he consults a rangefinder and tests the wind in order to select the proper ammunition load.

This is a little different from the way we do it. The duck hunting technique that my son and I have honed and perfected over the years is as follows: The day before duck season one of us remembers that tomorrow is opening day. We race to town to buy a duck license and a couple of boxes of whatever kind of shells are on sale. The next morning we blow the dust off our shotguns and get in an 18-foot-long shiny white canoe. We paddle out into the center of the slough. Sooner or later a couple of ducks will fly by. One will look down and say to the other, "Say, Harvey, what is that thing down there? Let's take a closer look. We've got nothing better to do. We can't go to our favorite place, because it's crowded with plastic ducks and concealed hunters." When the ducks get close enough, my son shoots them.

When I took my friend and his son hunting using my technique, his son got his limit in under two hours. He's going hunting again tomorrow, using his technique.

Some people never learn.

Prozac and Parts Stores

Well, I'm done with another harvest. Hopefully by the time this is published everyone else is done too. If you've farmed for any amount of time, you've had enough catastrophes hit you that it makes you bleed a little bit when bad luck befalls one of your neighbors, because you know exactly what it feels like. I'm feeling pretty chipper right now, but I won't completely relax until everyone's crop is in. There are a couple of fields I'm worrying about and I'm not even completely sure who farms them.

It was a struggle again, as usual. We had two hours of corn combining left with rain predicted when something in the innards of the combine started making a horrendous noise. It turned out to be nothing serious; "nothing serious" in combine repairs translated into a trip to Madison for parts and three hours of downtime. I finished in the dark with clouds rolling in to cover the moon. When I was unloading the last trailer, the auger stalled and I spilled about 100 bushels of corn on the ground before I could climb out of the bin. Compared to what might have happened, things went pretty well. I talked to a guy the other day who had rented a big combine so he could be sure to finish harvest early. He had used it for five hours when they ran a rock into the cylinder and had to quit work for two days to fix it.

Been there.

Done that.

Didn't like it.

My son had a great idea. You know how when you come to the counter in a supermarket there are all these trinkets like gum and combs to buy? Well, parts stores have the same thing. His idea was that next to the hitch pins and chain oil they could sell little convenience packs of Valium, Prozac and Tums. I don't think they would need any stimulants. Most farmers I see in parts stores around harvest time are already so frenzied you wouldn't want them to be any more awake. Especially if you are the parts man. I asked one of them if they had to take any special counseling classes in parts man school. He laughed and said no, but he often wishes he had. He told me that some guy will wake up and get in a fight with his wife before breakfast. He'll turn on the radio only to hear that the markets are dropping and in the mail he'll find a letter from the IRS. Then he will go out to work, some part will break on some machine, and he'll come into the parts store and drop the whole load on the poor parts man.

Wouldn't it be a lot simpler if the parts man could hear him out, then slide a couple of big capsules of some calming drug across the counter and say, "Here you go, Fred. Why don't you wash these down with a little decaf and our in-store masscusc will rub your temples while I go dig out one of those HG Mark 17 splined gears for you. I'll be back to give you the bill after we know for sure they've kicked in." With some soothing music in the background and a comfortable couch, the whole experience could be a lot more nurturing.

I'm willing to give it a shot.

Wintertime

Well, here it is, winter again. You would think we would learn. The weather was good for quite a while. We had our chance. We could have all loaded up and moved to Arizona, but no, we stayed, hoping that this year maybe winter wouldn't come. Now it is too late.

It is a little known fact, but the state line south of us is closed after Christmas. They let tourists out, but if someone shows up in a moving van, trying to sneak out permanently, they are turned back. I think the southern states do it as a way of pest control. You can't blame them. How would you like it if your state filled up with people too dumb to remember from March to October what winter in Minnesota is like? Come to think of it, our state is full of that kind of people.

I have no idea if this is true, being of the male persuasion, but I read somewhere that women's memories of childbirth are purposely dimmed by Mother Nature, the reason being that if they could remember clearly what it was like no one would ever have more than one child. As I said, I have no idea if this is true or not, but it kind of makes sense. I wonder if the same thing doesn't happen to people who live here all year round.

When the leaves start to change in the fall we think of the beauty, and the fun we had as kids playing in big leaf piles. We forget the hard, driving October rain that turns everything cold and gray and sends chills down your back. We breathe deeply the brisk air on the morning of the first hard freeze and smile at the feeling, but have to re-learn that any vehicle left outside will need all six windows scraped free of frost before we aren't a hazard on the road. When we get a couple of inches of fluffy snow in December we remember walking to church Christmas Eve with great big snowflakes falling past the streetlights. We forget that the reason we walked was because the car was stuck in the driveway.

It is easy to be nostalgic about big blizzards. Everyone has fond memories of being snugly inside the house while the wind howled outside, making cookies with the kids, drinking coffee and cooking good meals that you ordinarily would never have time to prepare. It is such a wonderful, sinful feeling to just do nothing, especially when there is nothing you can do about it because you are snowed in. On the other hand, I can remember being snowed in once when we hadn't had time to get to town and buy groceries. We lived on pork chops and water for three days.

I suppose it is just human nature to remember the good and gloss over the bad. Maybe it is what helps us keep our sanity and our hopes for the future. Still, I am already tired of the dry, cold air of winter. I can't wait until July when the sun beams down from a cloudless sky and the air is heavy with moisture. Or am I forgetting something?

Lutefisk

My wife made lutefisk for me the other night. What a woman.

It was a sacrifice for the entire family. Not only did the

kitchen smell but everyone had to sit at the supper table with me and watch me eat it. We almost lost one of the girls when I bumped a table leg and the lutefisk started to wiggle.

My background is mainly Norwegian, so I have had a lifetime to get used to the concept of lutefisk. My wife is mainly Irish. When she was growing up her family ate turkey, ham, and mashed potatoes for Christmas Eve dinner. The first Christmas we spent together she came to my parents house. We had our traditional oyster stew and lutefisk. She thought it was a cruel joke.

I've given lutefisk a great deal of thought. In my opinion, since Norwegians as a rule are nearly perfect, lutefisk was invented to give other nationalities some minor flaw to make fun of. Otherwise, the jealousy would be terrible. The only problem with that theory is that Swedes eat it also. Lets face it, there's no jealousy problem there. On the other hand, maybe a couple of thousand years of cold weather and leaky boats have ruined our taste buds.

This theory gains some support when you look at other cold-weather countries. Scotland, for example. Their national dish is called haggis. This is made of, and I'm not lying here, a sheep's stomach stuffed with, well, stuffed with the sort of things that a person who would cook a sheep's stomach in the first place would use for stuffing. This would appear seriously warped, except it does seem to blend in with other Scottish characteristics. Keep in mind, Scots invented golf and the men wear skirts and no underwear, an odd clothing choice for people who live in a drafty climate. Scotland has always had a reputation as a country filled with tough, pugnacious warriors willing to fight at the drop of a hat. Well, does this surprise you? How would you feel if on your day off you had to wander around a golf course in the rain wearing a skirt, then come home to a hearty meal of sheep's stomach?

Ireland is another country where it gets a bit chilly in the wintertime. I don't really know what the national dish of Ireland is. My understanding is that all they used to eat was potatoes, until some bug got in the potatoes and made them rot. Then everyone starved except for the ones who came to America, where they invented the concept of green beer on St. Patrick's Day.

Parts of Canada, of course, are very cold. More support for my theory I'm afraid. Tell me the last time you saw a cookbook entitled "Classic Canadian Recipes!" The only exception would be Quebec, except Quebec thinks it is part of France, which does have good food.

Eskimos, used to live on seal blubber. I rest my case.

Stables

I've been thinking, and all in all, I can think of a lot worse places to be born than a stable. They say it happened in a stable because there was no room at the inn. I've seen a dozen Christmas programs where the heartless innkeeper points his arm and orders the desperate family away, because he is full up. Maybe he wasn't so heartless. If you had to choose, which would you prefer? The hallway of a Thrifty Scot on a crowded weekend or a barn?

I'm not talking about one of my hog barns. There's nothing comforting about a modern hog barn. They may be clean, efficient, well-maintained; any number of adjectives like that come to mind. But nurturing? I don't think so.

No, I'm talking about the barns we used to have. When I was very young, the barn we had was probably not a great deal different from barns of a couple thousand years ago. There was a place to store hay and straw, stalls for animals, a couple of doors and probably a couple of windows for ventilation. Nothing complicated, but good enough for the purposes. I know Palestine is a lot further south than Minnesota, so I imagine it doesn't get nearly as cold in December. As I write this though, my son is in Kuwait sleeping in a tent and he says it gets down to freezing at night, so I'm sure some bedding was used. From all the talk about winnowing and thrashing in the Bible, I imagine the bedding was loose straw.

I'm sure it was dimly lit. Barns now are full of banks of fluorescent lights, but the barns I remember were all dim, and that was after electricity. I remember standing next to an older man at an auction once when they were selling kerosene lanterns for $115 each. He told me that the day he got electricity on his farm he had taken six of them behind his grove and thrown them as far as he could. He said, and I quote, "If you set them damn things on the floor you couldn't see to tie your shoe." I'm sure the lanterns in Palestine weren't any better, but dim is OK. In fact, babies prefer dim.

People might say, "But barns stink. Ewww!"

Well, no, actually they don't. Not if they are kept clean, and the animals aren't sick, and fresh straw is in every pen. They still smell of course, but it isn't a bad smell, just the smell of, well, of life. Babies smell, too, you know.

All in all, not so bad. It would have been scary of course, all births are scary, but it would have been warm, and quiet, with the soft sound of animals shifting in the darkness. There would have been people around who cared, and helped, and through one of the windows there would have been shining light from the stars.

Maybe only from one star.

Sometimes, one star is all you need.

New Year

Happy New Year. I hope your new year has gotten off to a good start. I myself have always wondered why in the world we have a new year's celebration in January. Leaving the celebration itself aside, which on a few occasions has left me feeling very old indeed, there is nothing new about January in Minnesota.

Think about it. Why January 1? The school year is half over. Any novelty that might have existed with new teachers, classes or books is worn out. Even if you have the type of children who leap out of bed eagerly to begin the school day, and I have heard that such children do exist, going to school in January is not quite as thrilling as it was in September.

There is certainly nothing new about the weather. Even though winter isn't supposed to start until December 22 (don't get me started on that) we've had weather that fits my definition of winter for two months, with about three months left to go. Our dog drools a lot, and if she stays in one place too long outside her jowls freeze to the ground and we have to chip her loose. This isn't fun for anyone involved, and it isn't what I would consider a favorable way to begin a new year.

The election was a couple of months ago, but the new people we elected don't start doing things for another three weeks. Granted, some of them are new to office, but if experience tells us anything, it tells us they'll probably be doing some of the same old things to us.

There is Christmas, of course. That is a very notable symbol of a new beginning, but really that is in December. I always get a big lift in my morale from the Christmas Eve service. It makes me feel like there is hope. But by January that feeling has started to evaporate. Half the toys you've given your kids are broken and you've spilled pickled herring on the tie you got from Aunt Edna. It is also time for the credit card bills to start showing up.

There are all the football bowl games of course. So, if you celebrate the New Year in the traditional fashion you spend the day in your recliner drifting in and out of a sugar coma, munching on more snacks than you've needed since you were twelve, while a bunch of teams you know very little about play a game in a much better climate than you're currently enjoying. It would be a lot more fun if the University of Minnesota was in a bowl game. I'm 42 years old, I don't know if I'll live that long.

January 1 you're supposed to turn over a new leaf, which for a lot of us means going on a diet. What wonderful timing. Everyone with ten minutes of spare time has been baking sweet stuff, there are leftovers filling the refrigerator already cooked, it is too cold to exercise outside, and we only have three hours of daylight so it feels like time for bed by 4:30 in the afternoon. I can feel the pounds dropping off already.

So there you have it. If you're a kid you have to go back to school. If you're an adult you're fat, tired, behind at work from the holidays, winter is less than half over and it's time to start worrying about bills, taxes, and what the new crop of politicians we elected are going to do to us.

I need some eggnog.

Education

I am a firm believer in education. Formal education, like chocolate, is a wonderful thing. Like chocolate, I've come to believe that too much of it is bad for your health and can ruin your complexion.

I've thought about this for many years, and it seems to me that the problem with too much formal education is that after a while you start thinking you know something. The danger is that as soon as you are fairly confident you have mastered a field, at that point your real education ceases.

I remember a guy I once met at a party. He was memorable because at the time he was working as a receptionist at a hospital and had started a campaign to get the rotary dial phones changed to push-button, because the old style was so hard on his fingers. We talked a bit and he told me he was looking for a different job. It turned out he had degrees in philosophy and religion. The only thing he was qualified to do was be a messiah. I mentioned that to him, but the potential downside to that sort of a career made it unappealing to him.

He sure was smart though. At the drop of a hat he could ramble on about various Germans and Greeks who were complete unknowns as far as I was concerned. I enjoyed talking to him because I know I don't know anything about that stuff, and by and large I'm always eager to learn about something I know little about. The truth is though, after a while he made me tired. His entire life had been spent in the world of books, and outside of that world he not only lacked knowledge, which is unfortunate but perhaps understandable, but he also had a contempt for anyone who did know something useful, like plumbing or carpentry.

I'm not sure when we got the distinction between a college degree and an education confused. It's kind of funny when you think of it. George Washington, Thomas Jefferson, Harry Truman and Abraham Lincoln between them didn't have enough of a formal education to get them hired as the second assistant secretary of carpet inspection, but the last time I checked they did a fairly good job in the field of government. On the other hand, you've got Henry Kissinger. Here's a guy with more education than you could shake a stick at. If he weren't homely as a mud fence he could be the poster boy for higher education. Nixon puts him in charge of negotiating with the North Vietnamese. Their first offer is that we should go away, and let them do whatever they wanted. After another three years of negotiation Bad Boy Hank gets the North Vietnamese to agree to his deal. His deal is that we would go away, let the North Vietnamese do whatever they wanted, and plus we offered to pay them a bunch of money to fix the stuff we blew up. In between times about half a million people got killed and enormous hunks of several countries were strewn around.

I qualify people by the desert island format. You know,

picture what it would be like to be stranded somewhere with a group of people, one of whom is the person you're talking to. Most of the people I'm fond of would do real well in a situation like that. I know people that a week after they floated ashore would have a power plant built out of seaweed and coconuts and would be working on domesticating wild pigs to pull a cart that they had hewed out of a palm tree log, using empty clam shells. On the other hand, my phone dialing double-majored buddy would have been explaining the fascinating group dynamics of desert island strandings until we all sank into a last starvation coma.

The truth is, in our society we've got plenty of people who can tell us what we've done wrong, and even more people willing to tell us how to do it next time. What we've got a real shortage of is people who can, and do, roll up their sleeves and actually do the work.

Heading South

I know some people who are spending the month of February down south. When they left I distinctly saw them rip off their rear-view mirror and throw it in a snowbank. Good riddance, I say. Let 'em scurry for sunshine and palm trees. Who needs 'em? We'll have plenty of fun right here in our winter wonderland.

Yeah, you're right. They wouldn't take me along when I begged. They threw me out when I hid in the trunk.

I'm starting to think the buffalo had it right. Back a hundred and fifty years or so, the plains had huge herds of buffalo.

They had no set territory, but just wandered over the plains grazing as they went. From what I have read, this wandering was a fairly random thing. Maybe so, but I can't help but think that when it got to be winter in Montana, the Dakotas and Minnesota, the buffalo herd decided to wander down to the Gulf Coast and dip their little hooves in some warm salt water for a change.

The people who were heading south told me that it had been "real cold in Arizona this year. It might not be any better down there than it is up here." Excuse me, unless they are going to Saskatchewan or Antarctica, pretty much any place has to be better than here.

Perhaps this sounds like I'm whining a bit. I have to do my whining on paper, because whenever I go to town and whine to people, it turns out the person I'm whining to has had a much harder winter than I have. That is so annoying. I will be telling a story to someone about how I had to go out and feed the pigs when it was -20, and then they'll tell me how their barn collapsed and now they have 300 sows sleeping in the basement of their house. I'll move on to someone else and tell them how it took me 35 minutes to drive the mile and a half between our farms, and they'll tell me how they had to crawl for eight miles on their hands and knees so they could find the road, while their six-year-old drove the car.

I could make up a more extravagant story to win sympathy. The problem with that is that then I'm tiptoeing a fine line between heroism and stupidity. It takes a little fun out of telling a story about how I battled through 10-foot tall snowdrifts for six hours in order to bring back fresh waffle flour to my family only to have the person I'm telling the story to say, "Geez, what an idiot. Why didn't you just stay home? Don't you realize you're a hazard to the whole community when you go out and drive around in bad weather?" Not exactly the reaction I'd hoped for.

There is a certain amount of truth to it though. I've always felt that most adventures are the result of poor planning.

This brings us back to those people headed down south. They were here all through January, the worst month of winter in living memory. Wouldn't it just serve them right if February was lovely and the weather down south was horrible? It could happen.

I hope they sit on a cactus.

Hell

I hope I go to heaven. I think of myself as a fairly good guy so I've got a shot at it, but it's not a sure thing. I really don't have any idea what heaven will be like, but I'm really clear on what hell would be.

If I awake after I die, and I'm greeted by a pleasant person with a nice smile who beams at me and says, "We'll get you settled in a jiffy; all you have to do is fill out a few forms first," I'll loosen my collar, look around, and say, "Gosh, it is warm down here, isn't it?"

I really hate filling out forms. If there is ever a revolution, I won't be lynching corrupt officials, or looting businesses, but I'll be first in line to burn down the carbon paper factories.

A long time ago, I borrowed some money from FmHA. (I don't owe them money any more, so I think it is safe to make fun of them. I hope so anyway.) This was back when interest rates were really high; I think the prime rate was around 18%, so they charged me a really high rate of interest. We got along fine for a while. Every December they would send me a bill and 20 pages of forms to fill out to prove I was still alive. Every year I would write out a check and fill out the forms.

After a few years, interest rates went down, and the banks and other lending institutions all lowered their rates. I went to talk to my friendly FmHA people about getting my rate lowered. After I filled out another 20 pages of forms, telling them everything except what color socks I wore, they told me they couldn't lower my rates. "Why?" I said.

"Because you've always paid your payment," they said. "If you had skipped some payments, then you would be a bad risk, and we could give you a better deal."

Right about here is where my head started to hurt. Most businesses give you a better deal if you pay your bill on time. Only the government could figure out a way to punish you for trying hard.

When December rolled around that year, I got my bill from FmHA along with the 20 pages of forms. I sent them their money, but threw away the forms. I was hoping a bad attitude would qualify me as a bad risk so they would lower my interest rate. They called me in January to remind me to fill out my forms.

"I threw them away," I said. "If you want them filled out, I'll leave my records on my desk and you can fill them out yourself." With an attitude like mine, maybe I'd even get free money.

No such luck. After threatening me a couple times, they sent someone out and he filled out the forms himself. This went on another seven years, until I paid them off. After the last payment, I got a couple pages of forms, sort of a farewell gift I figured.

I threw them away.

Girl Scout Cookies

We got our Girl Scout cookies last week. My wife and I each have to order separately now. She thinks we should open one box at a time, each have a cookie, then put the box away to save for a treat the next day. I can't believe it. What planet is she from? When your cookies are delivered, you should eat the first box while you're still writing out the check. And as for one cookie at a time, if you look at the design on the package of "Samoas" it is clear that you are meant to grab a whole row, five or six cookies, at one crack. You can pace yourself a little with the "Thin Mints" but any of the others, when served with a hot cup of coffee, disappear like spring snow, unless your dunking hand gets tired.

Now, I'm a believer in moderation, but every now and then a little slip is OK. Why not? It's not like the Girl Scouts come around every week. This is a once a year shot.

I read an article about a bunch of guys who were sitting around talking about their lives. These guys were all in their mid-forties, and were all sensible men. They had reached that age when you start to worry about yourself a little, and try to be more prudent. They took the skin off their chicken, they drank decaf instead of regular and they got plenty of sleep. They were sitting around, comparing diet tips and exercise regimens.

They congratulated each other on how sensible they had become. After a while the conversation started to drag a bit. There is only a limited amount of time you can spend talking about the benefits of canola versus sunflower oil.

One of the men told a story. When he was young, his father and his uncles would go to the butcher shop and buy the piece of meat that the filet mignon comes from. The whole piece, about twenty pounds of beef. It was a family ritual. They would coat the meat with a crust of salt a half inch thick to seal the juices in. They would roast this in an oven for about an hour. Then they would take it out of the oven and break off the salt crust. The meat would only be about half cooked. They would take a big cast iron frying pan and melt a pound of butter in it. When the butter was melted, they would slice the meat and fry it in the butter to the degree of doneness that each person preferred. Then the guy's father and his uncles would sit around eating the meat with lots of fresh bread and wine, and talk about guy stuff. When he finished the story, everyone sat in silence for a moment. Then one guy cracked. "By George, let's do it!" he said hoarsely. And they did, and they still do, once a year. It makes perfect sense to me.

Want a cookie? Take two.

Chaperone

I went as a chaperone on a band and choir trip last week. It was billed as an educational experience and it certainly was for me. I learned that I am really, really old.

To begin with, it was a bus trip. We got on the bus at 8:30 in the morning and got off the bus 17 hours later. There were a few short stops along the way, but they weren't long enough for me. It takes about ten minutes before my knees bend when I get up in the morning, even when I sleep in my own bed. When I'm trying to sleep sitting up in a bus, it takes me a lot longer to feel really limber.

It didn't seem to bother the students nearly as much. I don't understand why God gives teenagers so much energy. I mean, who needs it more? Wouldn't it make sense if the grownups got all the energy and teenagers got just enough so they could go to school, come home and do the supper dishes? Then they could go to bed and listen to their radios quietly for a few minutes before they got nine or ten hours of sleep to prepare them for the next school day.

It doesn't work like that at all. I've been in close proximity to 78 teenagers for five days, and as nearly as I can tell, they need about 15 minutes of sleep a day to function at peak efficiency. If they are provided with unlimited pizza, they can trim another five minutes off that.

I've got a confession to make. I like teenagers. Some scientists go up into the mountains of Uganda to study gorillas; some spend their time in the ocean filming dolphins or sharks. I study teenagers. They are never boring. I have been terrified, furious, annoyed, amused and frustrated around teenagers, but I've never been bored.

I've done a lot of traveling with groups of teenagers and there have been a few times when it has been a little tough. I won't give you any details. If you've traveled with a bunch of kids you can supply your own stories, and if you've never done it, you wouldn't believe me anyway. It's understandable, really. If you stand close enough to a teenager you can see the hormones boiling off and hear a faint hum of energy. That all has to go someplace. With some luck you can channel it into something useful and/or harmless, but it does have to go someplace. But you know what? Do an experiment. Write down a random list of 78 adults you know. Now look at the list and imagine being responsible for all their actions on a week long trip to another state. Scary, isn't it? Now imagine trying to handle all the complaints and demands from those same 78 people. By comparison, teenagers are easy.

A few years ago I was in charge of a dozen teenagers on a trip to the Cities. We were staying at the St. Paul Radisson and it took quite a while to get everyone settled down. I wandered down to the lobby about 2:00 in the morning and met the night manager going off duty. We chatted a bit and I told him that I hoped we hadn't been too much bother. He said, "Your kids were fine. I had a convention of accountants in here last week and they were throwing potted geraniums off the third floor balcony trying to hit the brass ashtrays in the lobby."

Isn't it interesting that no matter what dumb things teenagers do, adults come up with something dumber?

Come in from the Dark

Quite often I return to the house after dark. Sometimes I am just finishing my day's labor. Sometimes I have been doing bookwork out in my office. Usually it is because I want to check if any sows are giving birth and need assistance.

The farrowing barn is warm and moist, bathed with a dim light from dirty light bulbs, and full of the sounds and smells of animals and maternity.

Before pigs became domesticated, they would prepare for birth by finding a secluded spot and rooting up the undergrowth and dirt to make a nest. These instincts are still in effect. The difference is that in the wild only a couple of a sow's 10 or more piglets would survive, so I restrain the sow in a crate that keeps her from crushing her babies with her weight and house her in a controlled environment so the babies don't get chilled. It is efficient, but not particularly pleasant for all concerned. Restraint of any kind bothers me a little, but as a species we have known for 10,000 years that you can't have a farm without a fence.

Still, there is something viscerally satisfying about the farrowing house. When you come in, if there is nothing wrong, you can hear the soft grunts of sows encouraging their young to nurse, and the rustles and jostling of piglets jockeying for position. Shortly after birth each pig picks out a nipple and nurses only at that one. Over the next three or four weeks as they get bigger they crowd each other out of the way, causing no little disturbance.

I have been farming for over 20 years, and it would have been difficult to do for that long if taking care of animals didn't provide me with some level of satisfaction. I think these after-dark visits are perhaps more for my benefit than for the pigs.

Winter in Minnesota is a visible, palpable presence. When you open the door of the farrowing house after dark on a December or January day, there is an enormous shock to the system. Inside is warmth, birth, and growth. Outside is none of those things.

I don't like yard lights. I am not scared of the dark and I enjoy looking at the stars. After long negotiations with my family, I installed one over by the garage, but that is on the opposite side of the building site, so it sheds little light by the pighouse.

The first step away from the pighouse reminds me that I have moved into a different world. In the crisp darkness the stars gleam with uncanny brightness. When it is very cold the snow itself complains when I take a step. The cold air seems to fill my lungs more fully than warm air. When I take a deep breath it feels as if every pocket of stale air is expunged and purified.

I walk slowly across the yard, reveling in the feeling of knowing such a huge and implacable universe. One of my all time favorite quotes comes from C. S. Lewis's *The Lion, the Witch, and the Wardrobe*. When the children find out about Aslan, the great lion that rules the land, the beavers tell them about Aslan's strength and ferocity. One of the children inquires nervously "Is he—quite safe?" Mr. Beaver draws himself up indignantly and says " 'Course he isn't safe. But he's good."

The world I live in is indisputedly good. But it is not safe.

If I were to turn the other way and walk into the darkness away from the farm I would die. If some mischance were to befall me, for instance if I were to slip and hit my head hard enough to leave me unconscious for an hour, I would die. The winter would not care at all. This is not a theory. It happens, every year, to many people. Nature is not to be mocked, and any unwary foolishness can be punished harshly.

The windows of our house glow with a gentle yellow light. Sometimes there is a brief shadow as a member of my family moves through the light, but usually there is nothing except the warm welcoming glow. It is a wonderful sight, a reminder that even in this huge uncaring universe there is a place for me. One thing only is a mystery to me. Everything in this world that matters to me is inside that house. Everything that gives my life value and meaning is there, but still, there is always a faint reluctance to leave the cold and enter the light.

A Black Hills Lady. W. H. O'Gara, one-time speaker of Nebraska's House, wrote this true story of a horse he raised on the South Dakota/Nebraska border. He calls it poetry of nature, tragedy and romance as the farm horse triumphs as a racehorse in the Tri-state Fair.
9"×6"   12-X $8.95

Daniel and Agnes Freeman Homesteaders. On January 1, 1863, Daniel Freeman filed the first homestead in the United States. This book by his great-granddaughter Beverly S. Kaplan tells the story of not only his property near Beatrice, Nebraska, but of the nearly desert land, the pioneers and their struggle to make the "free land" a home, the first house, the railroads and the politics of the era.
8"×5"   187 pages   26-X $9.95

Frontier Steamboat Town. Author Glenn Noble chronicles the history of Nebraska City from the arrival of the steamboat "Amaranth" in 1846. The city's history is skillfully explained along with its role in the development of the state and westward expansion.
8½"×5½"   257 pages   35-9 $9.95

Havelock, Nebraska. Jim McKee and Ed Zimmer. Established in the late 1880s and incorporated in 1893, Havelock, Nebraska was soon home to a Burlington Railroad locomotive assembly and repair shop. In the twenties Havelock had become the home of the largest aircraft manufacturer in the world. This illustrated history tells the story of the village's growth and ultimate annexation by the city of Lincoln.
8½"×11"   96 pages   33-2 $12.95

How Cold Is It . . . ? Roger Welsch and Paul Fell have teamed up again with a collection of Great Plains tall tales about our amazing winters. Roger did the hard part by choosing 36 stories while Paul did all the work in providing nearly 100 hilarious cartoon illustrations.
8½"×5½"   101 pages   34-0 $6.95

In All Its Fury. The story of the Great Blizzard of 1888. This storm, which covered nearly a third of the nation, roared down from Canada at 50 miles an hour, dropped temperatures 36 degrees, and killed more than 1,000 people, is described through the eyes of survivors. These accounts of heroism and courage were collected by W. H. O'Gara of Laurel, Nebraska, in 1947.
9"×6"   343 pages   04-9 $9.95

The Lay of the Land: A View From the Prairie. Brent Olson. With hunger, love and poignancy, a philosopher farmer's elegant essays distill the essence of life in the Great Plains. Olson farms the land settled by his Norwegian immigrant great-grandparents and lives in the house they built. Savor his views on life one by one, or wolf them down at one sitting. This is soul-nourishing stuff. For fans of Garrison Keillor, Henry David Thoreau and Tom Bodett.
Due Fall 1998.   5¼"×7⅛"   36-7 $11.95

Innocents on Broadway. Flavia Waters Champe, Nebraska dance teacher and professional dancer, chronicles her adventures as a 19-year-old traveling coast-to-coast with a vaudeville company in the 1920s.
272 pages   0-939644-24-X $9.95

Liars Too. The second collection of "the best medicine" gleaned from Roger Welsch's *Nebraska Farmer* column titled "Liar's Corner." The tall tales and just plain ol' lies are the sort that kept pioneers sane and farmers laughing—often at themselves—for decades.
5½"×8½"   116 pages   32-4 $5.95

Lincoln: The Prairie Capital. This 124-page book by Jim McKee tells the history of Nebraska's capital city with interesting accounts, stories and hundreds of photos. McKee recounts Lincoln's past from the tiny village of 30 with "no water power, mines, fuel, nor other so-called natural advantages" to the modern city of nearly 180,000, punctuating historical facts and formalities with how-it-happened anecdotes.
8½"×11"   124 pages   07-3 $17.95

Lincoln Walking Tour Series: Haymarket Landmark District. A revised edition of Ed Zimmer's history and walking tour with maps, illustrations and suggested routes. Due 1998.
20-0

Lincoln Walking Tour Series: Wyuka Cemetery. An illustrated history and tour of Lincoln's state-owned cemetery noting famous and infamous "residents" from 1869 to the present. Due 1998.
21-9

Luther North, Frontier Scout. Jeff O'Donnell. The scouts, who made the frontier railroads and settlement possible, were "one of the most thrilling chapters of Nebraska history." The story of Luther North, as told here, was one of the most fascinating links in the winning of the west.
5½"×8½" 216 pages 10-3 $13.95

Miss Adams, Country Teacher. At age 18 on March 1, 1928, Treva Adams Strait began teaching in a one-room converted cowboy's shack 35 miles from town on the western Nebraska prairie. Award-winning author Strait tells the story of her early teaching career and predepression life in Nebraska in a fascinating narrative suitable for all ages.
6"×9" 25-1 $8.95

Nebraska Place Names was researched for 17 years by Elton Perkey. This completely indexed book first appeared serially in "Nebraska History" and has been completely corrected and brought up to date. Entries for each town and county include populations, dates of establishment and discontinuance as well as notes on the origin of site names.
8½"×11" 226 pages 19-7 $12.95

Nebraska, Where Dreams Grow. The fourth printing of Dorothy Weyer Creigh's 160-page paperback on Nebraska reminiscences from sodhouses and chautauqua to center-pivot irrigation. A delightful history of Nebraska told in terms of what people did in their everyday lives
8½"×11" 156 pages 15-4 $12.95

Nebraska's Five Seasons: The Best of Paul Fell. Lincoln *Journal-Star* cartoonist Paul Fell has collected over 100 of his favorite "Sketchbook" pieces taking on everything from Nebraska's winters, parking problems, dieting, home repairs, and Father's Day to Nebraska's own fifth season, "football."
8½"×11" 24-3 $8.95

Nebraskaspeak. Political cartoonist Paul Fell is at it again. This time he's put together a Nebraska dictionary of the English language. Find out how Cornhuskers pronounce 72 really tricky words like *Beatrice* (Bee-at-ris) and *nuclear* (nuke-u-ler).
5½"×8½" 17-0 $5.95

No Gun For This Lady! Lilya Wagner, former Vice President for Advancement at Union College in Lincoln, Nebraska, tells the amazing story of Hulda Roper, Lincoln's first policewoman.
89 pages $5.00

Oh Grandma, You're Kidding. Gladys Douglass recounts eighty years of memories of growing up in Nebraska, told in humorous and interesting detail. Covering everyday life in the Great Plains and how it was survived, 30 chapters include: Before TV and Radio; Woman's Work; Baked Beans on Washday; Riding the Train; Dollar Day At The Fair; Omaha's Easter Tornado; and Seeing Halley's Comet. A fascinating recounting for those who "remember when" or those unable to recall life before TV.
110 pages 00-6 $7.95

Omaha Tribal Myths and Trickster Tales. Roger Welsch. Over 70 Omaha Indian tales featuring "Trickster" in his many guises are retold with annotations at the end of each story. These fables will help the reader appreciate the rich culture of the Omaha well before "civilization" was forced on them by white soldiers and missionaries.
6"×9" 285 pages 11-1 $14.95

Pinnacle Jake + Pinnacle Jake's Roundup. As told to Nellie Snyder Yost. 84 years worth of vivid recollections from A. B. "Pinnacle Jake" Snyder on what cowboy life was really like at the turn of the century. J. Frank Dobie said it is "one of the best range books I have read . . ." Includes nearly 100 pages of new—never before published—pages of Great Plains range life tales.
8"×5" 340 pages 28-6 $12.95

Remember When. Over 100 vignettes of Lincoln history from Jim McKee's Lincoln *Journal* "Memories & Moments" column, collected with illustrations.
Due 1998. 23-5

Seems Like Old Times: The Big Bands of the Midwest. From 1935 to 1955 the midwest was home to dozens of small traveling dance bands. Vocalist, band member and director Loren Belker recounts how these regional groups came about, lived and became a part of the midwest scene in a fascinating format filled with dozens of photographs.
8½"×11" 131 pages 30-8 $16.95

Sod-House Frontier. History professor Everett Dick describes, in vivid detail, the everyday life of Nebraska, Kansas and the Dakotas from 1854 to 1890. This scholarly yet readable work contains much on the development of agriculture, towns and life on the plains frontier.
hardback 550 pages 38-3 $12.95

Sod Walls. The sod house has gone from being one of the most common dwellings in Nebraska to the point where only a few originals still stand. Great Plains folklorist Roger Welsch has told the story of soddies in over 100 photos and illustrations with a clear and interesting text.
6"×8" 208 pages 27-8 $12.95

Starkweather. Jeff O'Donnell. From December 1, 1957, when the murder spree began, to January 29, 1958, nineteen-year-old Charles Starkweather and his fourteen-year-old girl friend Caril Ann Fugate left a trail of 11 dead bodies. While Caril Ann Fugate was sentenced to life in prison, on June 29, 1959, Starkweather received the death penalty. This is their story.
5½"×8½" 31-6 208 pages $10.00

True Nebraskans. Lincoln cartoonist Paul Fell tackles the definition of a Nebraskan with such observations as: "True Nebraskans think a good auto sound system is one that plays 'There Is No Place Like Nebraska'," or "True Nebraskans listen to the noontime commodities reports . . . and understand what they mean."
8½"×5½" 18-9 $5.95

You Know You're a Nebraskan . . . Lincoln *Journal* political cartoonist Paul Fell and Nebraska folklorist Roger Welsch have teamed up to produce this laugh-filled collection with gems like: "You know you're a Nebraskan if your ancestors arrived on the Burlington instead of the Mayflower." This revised edition is a great gift for any native, displaced Nebraskan, visitor or anyone who can relate to a climate which may see +110 and −10 . . . on the same day.
09-X $5.95

SHIP TO:

Name _____

Address _____

City _____ State_____ Zip _____

All orders shipped postpaid. Nebraska residents add appropriate sales tax.

ISBN prefix is 0-934904

MAIL ORDERS TO:

LEE BOOKSELLERS
281 East Park Plaza
66th & "O" Streets
56th & Hwy. 2
LINCOLN, NEBRASKA 68505
(402) 467-4416
toll free 1-888-665-0999
e-mail leebooks@binary.net

350798